Contents

FOREWORD

Bullying in School:
The Need for an International Approach

David A. Lane
Professional Development Foundation London

'At school I don't succeed, I am daily taunted by on teacher, and my mates. I feel a deep sense of failure.'

After writing this letter to his parents, on the 24th April 1987, Roberto aged 15, took his father's gun and killed himself.

This was an Italian child, but it could have been a child anywhere. Several such tragic examples are mentioned by the contributors to this book, (including this one from Sergio Basalisco). Suicide is one outcome of bullying, although thankfully a rare one, but it is just the tip of a vast iceberg of misery experienced by millions of children every day.

Yet, as a number of the contributors point out, it has remained a hidden problem. It, like all children's issues, only emerges onto the public arena following a dramatic case or a scandal.

Scandinavian countries provide an exception, for there bullying is part of the public arena, but even there tragedy has played its part. Two young people took their lives in Norway in 1982 following longstanding bullying. Roland has argued that this led directly to the Norwegian Campaign Against Bullying.

Recently, cases have reached the media in the UK and have contributed to concern. Yet, media concern cannot be translated directly into action. Action requires knowledge based on research which in turn enables the concern to be translated into appropriate action.

Roland has argued that the move from thousands of isolated islands of personal grief to public action, must pass through stages of research and public concern. This process has happened in Norway, and Munthe describes the current state of Norwegian knowledge. In many other countries the problem has been, until recently, all but imperceptible to the scientific community, as Viera da Fonseca argues in her chapter. Such research as there is has been largely generated by the activity of individual concerned practitioners and a few academics. Mona O'Moore provides an overview of these efforts in the UK and Ireland.

BULLYING
An International Perspective

DATE DUE FOR RETURN

David Fulton Publishers
London
in association with the
PROFESSIONAL DEVELOPMENT FOUNDATION

David Fulton Publishers Ltd
2 Barbon Close
London WC1N 3JX

First published in Great Britain by
David Fulton Publishers 1989

British Library Cataloguing in Publication Data

Bullying, an international perspective
  1. Schools. Bullying
  I. Munthe, Elaine II. Roland, Erling 371.5'8

  ISBN 1-85346-115-6

Typeset by Chapterhouse, The Cloisters, Formby

Printed in Great Britain by BPCC Wheatons Ltd, Exeter

As Niek de Kruif points out, in Holland the interest dates largely from a book published by van der Meer in 1988. Following that, a flood of interest has emerged. But that flood of interest has also brought forth a flood of ideas without a research base to support them. Thus we have those who offer the advice to Dutch victims that they should get a big dog!

The interrelationship between private concern, public grief (generated by media interest) and research-led action is a complex one. The publication in 1988, of the first UK book on the subject, (Tattum and Lane, 1988, Trentham Books) produced extensive media interest. Yet that interest could not have been possible except for the background of tragic cases, such as those referred to by Elliott.

The way the media handled the first UK book provides an example of positive action. Several thoughtful articles have appeared and radio and TV stations have covered the material, but have had to ask the questions, how should we cover this material? What should we do next? The 'next' in some cases has included advice phones, resource 'factfiles', and follow up programming. Some serious attempts have been made to move beyond the immediate newsworthy story. It is to be hoped that the interest does not now just fade away. This pattern also marked much of the Norwegian coverage.

The time is right, therefore, for this previously unrecognised problem to move from the stage of private grief to the public agenda. To create an effective public agenda, requires a knowledge base. Given the international nature of this problem the lessons that can be learned should be shared. It is in that context that this book appears.

It is no coincidence that the first European conference on Bullying took place in Norway. That conference, (in 1987) sponsored by the Council of Europe, brought together individuals from twelve countries. Delegates agreed to go away and undertake further work and share information. This book is in part an outcome of that process. The original papers in this volume look at the emerging international knowledge base and alternative approaches to action that are beginning to happen.

Part 1. International perspectives on bullying?

Research into bullying owes a substantial debt to the work of several Scandinavian pioneers. The contributors to this book refer to the most notable such as, Heinemann, Pikas, Olweus, and Roland. They have given us theoretical perspectives and models of working which have been only slowly influencing other practitioners.

In spite of the debt, Scandinavian research has left us with certain difficulties. These include both the theoretical models and the contrast in emphasis on work with victims and bullies rather than on the school as a whole. This book will consider both of these issues but will concentrate on the broader perspective to intervention which has increasingly been influencing work throughout Europe.

The first problem concerns the definition of the act. Heinemann originally reported on an activity he called 'mobbing', referring to a group attack on an individual who had disturbed the group's ordinary activity. Later work such as that of Olweus has referred to both individual and group action. The inclusion of psychological or physical threat in definitions of bullying also raises problems since there are established sex differences for these types of bullying as Munthe points out.

Pikas presents his concerns over confusion in terms. It is, he argues, not simply a matter of academic interest, for it leads to quite different treatment options. Munthe, discusses the theoretical difference but also points out that the overuse of the terms can lead to a down-grading of concern. Suddenly everything is mobbing or bullying and therefore it does not matter anymore. This theoretical argument has very real consequences for children's lives.

The intention of the aggressor, and belief of the victim, is considered a key aspect by some researchers in the UK (See O'Moore's chapter) and therefore the social process by which the phenomenum is labelled becomes important. Several contributors to this book stress the importance of the social context.

This confusion over terms has also led to difficulties in determining the level of such activities.

The answer will depend on how the theoretical perspectives are viewed. Are we to separate group violence and call that 'mobbing' and individual violence and call that 'bullying', or are we to view them as part of one set of social aggression in which a dominant individual or group intends and causes distress to another. Should we be concerned with actual incidents or the fear of being bullied.

Establishing the level, type, and duration of bullying has not proved easy even in the well-financed research studies in Scandinavia. Figures reported there vary widely as Munthe reports in her chapter. The figures reported from Italy and Spain also point to the difficulty. If we include children's fears of being bullied, then as Elliott's paper demonstrates, this is a major concern. However, distinguishing between fear and events might be important and may require different approaches to intervention.

The different percentages reported in this volume should not hide the misery of the children involved. Munthe in her chapter, refers to 80,000 Norwegian children. Tattum has referred to 870,000 children in England and Wales. The reader may care to calculate what a 10% figure would mean for their own country. The estimates which emerge from various authors suggest that rates vary between countries. The UK, for example, seems particularly prone to bullying, but differences in methodology make such comparisons impossible. Yates and Smith, in their chapter report the first attempt to obtain UK data using the same methodology as that used in the Scandinavian studies. They argue that there are about three times as many victims and twice as many bullies in their UK sample as in the Norwegian studies. As they state, there is no room for complacency. It is to be hoped that their findings stimulate further international comparisons.

Who, then, might be at risk? It could be anyone, but the research reported here has gradually provided us with a better understanding of the problem.

If in fact bullying is a complex social labelling process, then understanding its causation requires more than looking at bullies and victims. A broadly based model of bullying behaviour is beginning to be possible. Action needs to follow that understanding.

Part 2. Approaches to dealing with bullying?

Stephenson and Smith (cited by O'Moore) state that 25% of teachers feel that it is sometimes helpful to ignore the problem although the majority of children look to teachers to act. Given the misery that many thousands of children endure for several years of their lives we cannot afford to take an ostrich like position on bullying. This tendency is also noted by contributors to this volume, and it can lead to calls for something or anything to be done. This is not likely to be helpful.

A number of possibilities do exist. Besag has looked at the problem of vulnerable children and has considered both prevention and intervention.

Priest provides an overview of the techniques he has found useful in his work. His contribution effectively describes the need for varied approaches to work with different problem areas and the way in which individual practitioners, in the absence of national guidelines, have attempted a careful approach to intervention.

Elliott introduces her highly successful Kidscape model. This addresses the problem by teaching children the skills to be safe. It is the most widely used method in the UK and similar techniques are extensively used in the USA and Canada.

Pikas makes the important point that work with mobbing, that is group violence, requires special skills. The pioneering techniques he describes have proved highly successful, although he points out that some children may need individual work. The appearence of his common concern method in English will greatly contribute to our knowledge.

Walker provides the broader perspective by placing bullying in the context of the cooperative classroom. He describes the work of those in peace education in the USA, and Europe who have tried to develop techniques for the non-violent resolution of conflict.

That perspective is also reflected in the chapters by da Fonseca, Garcia and Perez. They point to the role of the social education curriculum and the key place of the form tutor. The tutor model, has increasingly influenced many school systems, and its role in dealing with bullying may be crucial. Basalisco and de Kruif also stress these points.

In conclusion, Roland makes an appeal for a systems-based approach which provides a framework for understanding bullying and through that integrating the varied approaches within one structure.

Numerous programmes by teachers working with individuals, groups, curriculum approaches and policy changes have started to emerge internationally. These show both the breadth of concern and the range of methods adopted in different countries.

There is now an emerging trend. We all share concern with awareness of the problem and careful work with bullies (or mobbers) and victims. More recent work points to the greater emphasis on empowering the victim, and the involvement of parents, community responsibility and the role of the academic and pastoral curriculum. In fact the emergence of a community response is beginning. In many ways the origins of such a policy lay with both ends of the original Scandinavian dimension. But such research can greatly benefit from the broader perspective now emerging from an international comparison of data.

Bullying is an international phenomenon. Concern has been expressed in cultures as diverse as those of Japan, the USA, Europe, in fact in all parts of our world. It is a subject on which an international perspective is of value and has already proved to be so.

One theme is perhaps shared by all those working in this field. Children, parents and teachers are entitled to live without fear in their school. It is for the school to take action through establishing a policy which creates an environment in which all feel valued and safe.

Bullying research is still in its infancy. If this international problem is to be overcome, it requires international cooperation.

PART 1

International Perspectives on Bullying

CHAPTER 1

Bullying in Britain and Ireland: An Overview

Astrid Mona O'Moore

'We all used to pick on him
He used to stand there and let us
We called him scabs
He was ugly beyond words
I hated him
He used to slaver and spit when he spoke
We used to call him names, bad names, horrible names.
Some teachers hated him
They said he was disgusting
Some said it was disgusting the way we picked on him'

Geoffrey Proudlock (1985)

Is there anyone who has not encountered such tales of bullying, taunting or teasing? Many, undoubtedly, recognise the considerable anxiety, suffering and misery that is so often associated with bullying. Yet it is not uncommon for people to regard bullying as a natural process, part of the inevitable and turbulent process of growing up. The common perception is that by enduring it and fighting back, boys and girls are toughened up and then better prepared for life.

It is only in the last 15 years or so that bullying has become a subject of scientific research. Most of the empirical data to emerge so far has, however, come from Scandinavian countries and Finland who have recognised bullying as a problem in their schools. A climate of serious concern on bullying has, however, not yet surfaced in other European countries. This very much became apparent at the first European teachers' seminar on 'Bullying in schools' held in Norway, August 1987 (O'Moore, 1988). In the United Kingdom and Ireland, for example, what has recently captured the major attention of teachers, school authorities, psychologists, sociologists and the media is the dramatic increase in the stress and strain on teachers and headteachers and the problems of indiscipline or disruption in the classroom.

The object of the present chapter, is therefore, to review the bullying situation in the United Kingdom and Ireland in the hope that it might stimulate greater awareness and interest and lead to the initiation of further research. Firstly the reported incidence of bullying will be discussed. Secondly the personal and background characteristics of both bullies and victims will be detailed and finally some of the approaches to prevention and treatment will be reviewed.

I. Incidence

Caroline St. John-Brooks (1984) reported that it is almost impossible to tell exactly how much bullying goes on in the United Kingdom because of the mixture of secrecy and exaggeration which surrounds bullying. She states 'now and again an example surfaces – a persecuted child commits suicide or plays truant or runs away – but for the most part bullying is an underground activity'. Violence in school, she writes can be anything from name-calling, teasing, sexual taunts, rough treatment of younger children, frequent fighting, protection rackets, harassment on the way to and from school through to the extremes of individual persecution and racial attacks'. Indeed, Darking (1987) reported that pilot work for the Kidscape Primary Kit revealed that bullying was one of children's main worries. Out of 4,000 children, 38% had been bullied badly or frequently enough to be very upset by it. Taylor (1987) furthermore, revealed that bullying causes parents more anguish than any other school problems.

Reid (1984) noted a relationship between truancy and bullying in schools. He discovered from his research into truancy and absenteeism in South Wales that no fewer than 15 percent and 19 percent in his sample respectively claimed that they first missed school and later continued to miss school for reasons associated with bullying. One boy, for example, started to miss school when he failed to pay a fine of 2p a day imposed on him by his classmates. This small sum was payable as protection money. If the sum was not paid, the pupil was bullied until such time as the payments started again. It is to be noted that more boys than girls were influenced by acts which they described as bullying. Reid also found that extortion was a popular method. He points out, however, that it is unlikely that the relationship between bullying and persistent absenteeism would be so high in many schools in different parts of Britain. Even in South Wales, he adds, 'such rumblings and undercurrents are unusual'.

Measor and Woods (1984) in their book 'Changing Schools': Pupil perspectives on Transfer to a Comprehensive suggest that bullying certainly comes high on the list of most children's anxieties about secondary school. But again, how much is myth and how much is based on realistic perception is not known.

There are, however, some British estimates. Mills (1976) in an exhaustive study of seriously disruptive pupils aged thirteen to sixteen years in 61 secondary schools in an L.E.A. found that bullying had a rate of 8 per thousand pupils. Two years later, Lowenstein (1978) reported an incidence of five percent among boys aged eleven to sixteen. The school population in the schools studied is shown in Table 1. It should be noted that the area studied was predominantly middle class.

Table 1.1: LOWENSTEIN (1978). The school population in the schools studied.

TYPES OF SCHOOL	NUMBERS	MALES	FEMALES
INFANT	1762	964	798
JUNIOR	1951	1072	879
SECONDARY	2061	822	1239
TOTAL	5774	2858	2916

The incidence of bullying varied depending on the age and sex of the children. See Table 2. ~ *where* ?

Table 2 further shows that the most observable forms of bullying were physical attacks on other children. There was also a greater amount of

Table 1.2: LOWENSTEIN (1978) Types of bullying predominantly observed and percentage of bullies identified in the population studied for each age group.

TYPES OF BULLYING	BOYS AGES			GIRL AGES		
	5-7	7-11	11-16	5-7	7-11	11-16
Physical and vicious attacks	3	9	29	0	2	7
Verbal Attacks	1	4	7	0	3	6
Severe but subtle psychological bullying	0	1	5	0	0	5
TOTAL	4	14	41	0	5	19
Percentage of Population	0.4	1.4	5.0	0	0.6	1.5

bullying among boys than girls. As is seen, girls were more likely than boys to use verbal and psychological types of bullying behaviour.

John and Elizabeth Newson (1984) in their latest examination of their longitudinal study on the upbringing of 700 Nottingham children, found that 26 percent of the mothers were aware that their children were being bullied at school. Four percent were seriously bullied. Few mothers on the other hand, admitted that their own children were bullies.

Stephenson and Smith (1987, 1989) recently published results from a study on bullying involving 49 teachers of 1,078 final year primary school children attending 26 schools in North-East England. Their findings indicated that bullying was a common occurrence. Twenty-three percent of the children were involved in bullying as either victims or bullies. The authors state that 'if bullying is as common in all primary school year groups then in a local authority with a primary school population of 47,000 children, around 11,000 children would be involved in the phenomenon'. The finding that the majority of bullies had started bullying a year or more previously and that the majority of the victims had been subjected to bullying for a year or so, again suggested that the problem does not sort itself out. A significant finding in the above study was that bullying was found to occur much more frequently in some schools than others. In three schools there was said to be no bullying at all among the final year children while in one school, over 50 percent of the year group were reported to be involved. Bullying tended to be more prevalent in the larger schools and in schools which had larger classes although the differences were not statistically significant. Differences in school policy were detected in schools with a high incidence of bullying as compared to schools with a low incidence. For example, in all but one of the schools with a low incidence of bullying 'the teachers expressed articulate, considered and also purposeful views on bullying which emphasized the need for prevention whereas this was less apparent in the high bullying schools'. Stephenson and Smith, furthermore, noted that bullying was more common in schools located in socially deprived areas. The authors, therefore, comment that 'in this context, it is of note that all the children involved in bullying, both the bullies and the victims are a fairly disadvantaged group'. However, it was noted that the highest score on the measure of deprivation together with the largest class size of all the schools was in fact a low bullying school. Another significant finding was that Stephenson and Smith identified not just two groups of children, i.e. bullies and victims but their data suggested that there were in fact 5 distinct groups: (1) victims: 7 percent of the children fell into this group; (2) provocative victims: a small subset (17 percent) of the victims above;

(3) bullies: one in ten of the sample were described as bullies; (4) anxious bullies: a small number of the bullies above (18 percent); mostly boys, were described as anxious bullies; (5) bully/victims: six percent of the total sample both bully others and are themselves bullied. The characteristics of these individual groups will be described later.

Arora and Thompson (1987) asked 12 to 14 year olds in a 'small comprehensive school with a mixed socio-economic intake' to define incidents which characterised bullying. The children then at a later date reported how many such incidents they were involved in during the previous week to being questioned. The most striking finding was that of the fourteen year old boys 50 percent said that someone tried to kick them at least once during the previous week, and 36 percent of them reported that someone had threatened to break something of theirs. Furthermore 19 percent of the twelve year old boys stated that other children demanded money from them and for 5 percent of this group this last incident had occurred more than once during the week in question. As the children had only to record bullying incidents for one week prior to participating in the survey, the extent to which the unfriendly incidents reflect longterm persecution or harassment which is at the heart of bullying remains uncertain. It should also be noted that Arora and Thompson found that only a minority of children were made unhappy by the 'bullying activities'. The authors, therefore, are of the opinion that there appears to be 'a continuum of acceptable violence which a large minority of children experience at one time or other, but which is minimised in effect by the operation of peer group processes except for a proportion of that group who are typically victims and who are made unhappy by having to cope with bullying peers'.

In Ireland there have also been some recent studies all of which have used a definition of bullying similar to the Scandinavian researchers, Roland (1983) and Olweus (1978) (i.e. bullying is longstanding violence, mental or physical, conducted by an individual or a group and directed against an individual who is not able to defend himself in the actual situation).

In a study restricted to examining bullies only, Mitchel and O'Moore (1987) sampled 24 regular primary school teachers in charge of a total of 720 pupils and reported an incidence of 6 percent. Byrne (1987) examined an urban Post-Primary school for boys with about 600 students ranging from 12 to 18 years and disclosed an incidence of 5.3 percent victims and 4.9 percent bullies. A year later Hillery and O'Moore (1988) examined the incidence of bullies and victims in four Dublin primary schools. The study comprised 783 children of 7–13 years of age. Overall 10.5 percent of the children were involved in serious bullying, that is 2.5 percent were serious bullies and 8.0 percent were seriously bullied. Serious bullying implies bullying or being bullied once a week or more often. These figures indicate an incidence that is twice as high as in Norway where a 5 percent incidence of bullying inspired their Department of Education to launch a national campaign.

The findings from Hillery and O'Moore showed, moreover, that as many as 43.3 percent have occasionally bullied other children and that 55 percent have been bullied occasionally. Indeed 20.8 percent of the total group of children expressed fear in coming to school as a result of bullying, 2.6 percent of whom expressed a strong fear. Almost all the children (92.8 percent) stated that something should be done to curb the problem of bullying in their schools.

Boys it was found were more prone to bully others and be bullied, a trend which is consistent with other studies. For example, the present study revealed that 13.3 percent more boys than girls were bullied, 6.8 percent seriously so. It must be emphasized that these figures are based on the pupils self-ratings, teacher ratings having yet to be analysed. Roland (1989) has reason to believe that girls are less willing than boys to answer truthfully to questions concerning their involvement in violent inter-actions.

It was noticable that the incidence of bullying in both the primary and secondary schools in Ireland was greatest in the remedial classes. Mitchel and O'Moore (1987) found that among the primary school children 16 percent of the children in the special classes were bullies. This compared with 5 percent in the regular classes. Similarly Byrne found that 13 percent of children from the remedial classes in the secondary school were victims and 9 percent were bullies as compared to 5 percent victims and bullies in the regular classes. In Hillery and O'Moore's study a distinction was made between children attending special classes full-time and those in regular classes but receiving remedial teaching. While more 'remedials' were involved in bullying than the non 'remedials', it was among the full time special class children that the highest incidence of bullying was found. Namely 68.6 percent of the children bullied others, 2.9 percent of whom bullied seriously while 77.2 percent were bullied, of whom 11.5 percent were seriously bullied. Incidences of equally high magnitude have also been found among children with emotional and behavioural difficulties (Stephenson and Smith, 1989; Lane, 1989).

Bullying in Dublin schools did not appear to be linked to 'disadvantaged children' as tended to be the case in Stephenson and Smith's study. For example, no relationship was found between socio-economic status and bullying in either the studies of Mitchel and O'Moore (1987) and Byrne (1987) or Hillery and O'Moore (1988) who found bullying to be most widespread in the school which had the second highest intake of children with professional and managerial parents. It should be noted, however, that this school was also the largest in the sample with 475 pupils. The two schools with children of predominantly lower socio-economic status were the smallest schools in the study. While these results may reflect a motivational distortion factor, they may, on the other hand, point to a difference in attitudes to aggressive behaviour or to a difference in school policy. It is hoped that teacher ratings and the children's personality assessments, and information about school organisation and ethos which are presently being analysed, will throw further light on this matter.

In contrast to many other European countries, schools both in Great Britain and Ireland are very varied. They can be predominantly middle-class or working class, single-sex or mixed, boarding or day, primary or secondary, selective or comprehensive, denominational and inter-denominational. The limited research reported together with anecdotal evidence and case studies on bullying have shown that no type of school is immune. However, there is certainly convincing evidence to show that aspects of school organisation and 'ethos' in the British Isles contribute markedly to the frequency of disruptive incidents. (Pringle, 1973; Hargreaves et al., 1975; Tattum, 1982). The National Children's Bureau (1977) in their Highlight on Violence, Disruption and Vandalism in Schools, point out how violent and disruptive behaviour has been linked with a curriculum which places too little emphasis on individual, non-academic achievement and too much on competition. In such schools, pupils unable to achieve academic distinction turn to bullying and disruption as a way of gaining attention and status. Streaming aggravates this situation. Neil Frude (1984), makes reference, for example, to teachers' pets as frequent targets of contempt for pupils who feel themselves to be out of favour. To be favoured or judged to be courting favour can be perceived as an offence and is likely to bring contempt and retribution.

Heavy and inflexible use of school rules have also been associated with poor behaviour in class (Pringle, 1973). Indeed relationships between teachers, such as hostility and lack of rapport between staff-members can adversely influence the environment of the pupils. Frude (1984) refers to research which suggests that a lack of consensus regarding the overall approach to management can lead to major inconsistencies in 'toleration limits', with the result that quite different expectations regarding behaviour are transmitted to the pupils.

Although bullying behaviour is not synonymous with disruptive behaviour, there is some research which has shown that disruptive children are often anti-social, exhibiting aggression towards other children and sometimes staff, in bullying, refusal to cooperate, disobedience, stealing, lying and tantrums (Mills, 1976; Lawrence et al., 1984). Therefore, where there is a growth in disruption one might expect a corresponding growth in bullying. Existing statistics on the extent of violent and disruptive behaviour are limited by inexact record keeping and problems of definition. Laslett (1977) indicated however, that it is more common in secondary than in primary schools, among boys than among girls, in urban than in rural areas and among low ability disadvantaged pupils.

McNamara (1975) found an average of 4 percent of pupils to be seriously disruptive in class, with a further 10 percent occasionally disruptive. A number of local authorities maintain that figures have increased since that time, and that there is substantial under-reporting of fairly serious incidents (Frude and Gault, 1984). One must take note, however, that many local authority studies found both violent and disruptive behaviour to be concentrated in a few schools (National Children's Bureau, 1977).

In Northern Ireland, where children daily hear, if not see results of violence, one would perhaps expect a 'trickle-down effect' in the schools of the increased violence in society. Wilson and Irvine (1978) have reported a relationship between violence in the North of Ireland and conduct disorders in children. Conduct disorders included fighting, bullying, destructiveness, insolence, stealing and truancy. It was hoped therefore that the most recent report on discipline (Department of Education for Northern Ireland, August 1987) might have thrown some light on bullying. An increase in the incidence of indiscipline was, however, reported by 45 percent of the principals and 59 percent of classroom teachers. However, bullying did not attract any particular attention in spite of the fact that all headteachers were surveyed. Perhaps this should come as no surprise as according to Caroline St. John-Brooks (1985), Her Majesty's Inspectors in the United Kingdom never mention racial bullying in their reports on schools. Yet, it is on record that when Sir Keith Joseph was Education Secretary, he condemned racial bullying in a speech given in Reading, March 1983. Again the Runnymede Trust, in their Bulletin of October 1984 gave several examples of Asian children being attacked and injured. It is encouraging to learn that systematic efforts are presently being made to understand more fully and counter the adverse effects of racial harassment (Tattum, 1989).

As in Scandinavia, efforts have been made at national level in Japan to identify and curb bullying. The police, for example, have been called in to help catch the bullies by providing special phone lines for pupils, parents and teachers. Why then is bullying surrounded by under-reporting, complacency or even denial in Great Britain and Ireland? The author believes that reasons vary depending on whose interests are at stake. Firstly, the pupil, he helps bullying to go undetected because of fear of reprisals. There is also the social pressure to cope. In our status-conscious society there are many children who would rather not admit that they are underdogs, or bottom of the pecking order. Furthermore, telling tales in Great Britain and Ireland is taboo. Society after all admires the strong and offers minimum support to the weak. Attitudes such as these have been clearly illustrated in a report published by the Birmingham branch of the National Association of School-masters/Union of Women Teachers (NAS/UWT, 1987) on sexual harass-ment of teachers by pupils. In this article it was learned that *of the 45 percent* of male teachers, who reported one or more direct experiences of sexual harassment, only two had disclosed the matter to the school head or governors. The men, it turned out felt under considerable social pressure to 'cope'. Otherwise they felt they would be viewed as prudish, weak, or unmanly. This situation is remarkably similar to that of the bullied. Ironically the report by NAS/UWT went on to say that, 'it is a damning indictment of the system in which we operate that victims of abuse of this nature feel they have to suffer in silence'.

The union, therefore, called for each local authority to establish an independent counselling service devoted to offering advice and support for victims of harassment. The questions could be posed: Why have teachers not been calling for similar actions for their pupil victims of bullying? Is it that they do not see bullying face on?

The studies available indicate that teachers were aware that bullying takes place in their schools. Perhaps they have been powerless to do any-thing about it or have possibly been so wrapped up in their own teacher-stress that they have been unable to accommodate pupil stress. It is also possible that bullying does not make the teachers' life unpleasant nor interferes with his academic aims as is often the case of the insolent and disobedient child. Coupled with this is, of course, the often heard atti-tude that children have their own social system and should sort them-selves out. In other words, the victim will toughen up and learn to cope.

In addition to pupils and teachers, headteachers and school authorities are also party to the social pressure to cope. There may, for example, be a reluctance to admit to problems of bullying as this can reflect badly on 'the good name of the school' and on their own reputation as administrators. Heads might also judge that such a 'call for help' may be regarded as an 'admission of defeat' and weaken their perceived competence in the eyes of pupils, parents, colleagues and authority administrators. Arguments such as these have all been advanced to account for the bias suggested in reporting the incidence of disruptiveness.

In conclusion, the material available from the British Isles suggests that bullying goes on in British and Irish schools but to what overall extent is an uncertain matter. If we use the statistics which are available on violence and disruption in schools as guidelines then the picture which emerges from the British Isles leaves no room for complacency as it may represent only the tip of the iceberg. As in the words of the Hampshire Report on Pastoral Care (1975) there is no such thing as 'acceptable bullying'.

II Personal and background characteristics of bullies and victims

Lowenstein (1978) was one of the earliest investigators in England to attempt a 'micro-analysis' of the bully. He noted that the identification of bullies was not always unanimous. Teachers did not always agree on who were the bullies, indicating that bullying was on a continuum with normal aggressive or domineering behaviour. Teachers themselves viewed bullying differently, due to their own orientation and experience with particular children. Lowenstein (1978) therefore applied strict criteria before selecting bullying children for closer examination. Thus the study merits some attention. Lowenstein found that the bullies in his study were more likely to be hyperactive and disruptive in classs, and had higher neuroticism scores than their controls. Moreover, they had lower IQ's and were below average in reading achievement. Lowenstein also found that bullying children of either sex were more likely to have parents who had marital problems and conflicts at home; been bullies themselves; had a poor approach to rearing children, i.e. inconsistent, overstrict and over permissive and who had a lack of values relating to sensitivity to other people.

In a later study of thirty-two victims of bullying, (strict criteria having once again been applied) Lowenstein (1978a) found bullied children also had distinct physical characteristics and personality traits which distinguished them from the non-bullied child. Social and background features appeared to influence the possibility of being bullied.

Social skills and the capacity to communicate, to be popular and show interest in others were likely to mitigate against being bullied. Moreover, children were less likely to be bullied if they were physically robust, extraverted, socially sensitive, unselfish, flexible, conforming to group norms, rewarding, unaggressive, non-attention seeking and modest.

Lowenstein's findings in respect of the victims were very similar to the Scandinavian and Finnish results, i.e. the victim is insecure in his social relations and is physically weak (O'Moore, 1988). Lowenstein, did not, however, distinguish between the provocative and the passive victim as did Olweus (1978). If this distinction is ignored it might so easily cloud results. Lowenstein, for example, found his controls to be less aggressive than the victims, a finding which is in the opposite direction of what one would expect of the passive victim. Indeed Stephenson and Smith's (1987) data of primary school children clearly distinguishes the passive victim from the provocative victim. Whereas the majority of their victims, as in the Scandinavian literature, were passive, weak and ineffective individuals, the provocative victims were rated as more active, assertive, confident and physically stronger than other victims. They were not only easily provoked but they also provoked other children. Whereas most victims actively avoid aggressive situations, these children were found to actively seek these out. In addition a large number of these children frequently complained to their teachers that they were being bullied.

Stephenson and Smith believe that because these children actively provoke the bullying to which they are subjected they are a particularly vulnerable and problematic group.

Equally worrying were the small number of anxious bullies. Whereas they found the majority of bullies shared the characteristics of the Scandinavian bullies, i.e. confident, assertive, physically strong, reasonably popular, the anxious bullies were rated as lacking in self-confidence. In fact, they were found to be the least confident of all the groups. More of these children were reported to have problems at home and they were less popular with their classmates than other bullies. Their teacher described them as having fewer likeable qualities than the other groups and they also had the poorest school attainments and poorest concentration of all the groups.

Stephenson and Smith believe that only the small group of the 'anxious bullies' were in many ways similar to the popular stereotype of the bully, i.e. 'all bullies are cowards'. They also emphasise that it is this minority who represents the bullies so often' portrayed in fictional stories as being 'ignorant oafs' who give vent to repeated experience of frustration and failure at school by wreaking their vengeance on the 'class swot'.

The group of children who both bully others and were themselves bullied were found by Stephenson and Smith to be exceptional in that these children were rated as 'least popular' with other children. Like provocative victims they are easily provoked and frequently provoke others but are also physically stronger and therefore more able to assert themselves. Stephenson and Smith speculated that the hostility which is directed by these children towards their victims 'is fuelled by their own experience of being victimised in a different context and situation'.

The studies from Ireland also found many distinguishing features between bullies, victims and non-bullied children.

Mitchel and O'Moore's (1987) study of 720 primary school children, for example, distinguished between the bullies in the regular classes and remedial classes. Whereas 43 percent of the bullies in regular classes were considered popular children none of the bullies in the remedial classes were rated as popular. It may well be that this latter group were the 'anxious bullies' described by Stephenson and Smith.

The Dublin children's personalities which were based on the teachers' spontaneous or free description of the children as well as their ratings on the Rutter Behaviour Questionnaire, indicated that for the most part the bullies were unhappy, troubled children. Of the 23 bullies in the regular classes on whom the questionnaires were returned, 19 had scores above 9 which indicates a behavioural problem. In contrast, a control group of non-bullies suggested that only 2 children had behavioural problems.

Further analysis of the questionnaires indicated 15 of the 19 bullies with behavioural problems were classified as anti-social. Three bullies were neurotic and the remaining one undifferentiated i.e. had antisocial and neurotic scores which were the same. The cognitive abilities of the bullies were predominantly average or below average. Examination of the children's social background revealed that 77 percent of all the bullies studied were regarded as having a social or environmental background which contributed to their bullying behaviour. Adverse factors in their background included broken homes, alcoholism, poverty, assertive pugnacious parents, lack of maternal affection, inadequate and inconsistent discipline.

Byrne's study is of further significance in that he examined secondary school boys (both victims and bullies aged between 12–17 years) attending a single-sex school. No study of bullying in Ireland and Great Britain to date has concentrated solely on a single-sex school. Byrne found that whereas there were no significant differences in the level of intelligence between the bullies, victims and the control group, the bullies were found, as in other studies, to be physically stronger and more willing and capable of retaliating than the other groups. In comparison to both the victims and the normal controls the bullies were rated as the most popular group by their peers.

It is to be noted that the victims were assessed by their teachers as being of 'unusual appearance' to a greater extent than the controls and the bullies. It was also found that both victims and the bullies had abnormal speech patterns compared to the control boys. Speech in this context referred to mumbling, muttering, or particularly high or low voices. It also emerged that a large majority of both victims and bullies (94 percent in each case) had abnormal external physical characteristics. This compares with 67 percent of the control group.

Teacher ratings of personality characteristics indicated that bullies in contrast to the victims were excessively dominating, aggressive, boastful, attention-seeking for reward and demanding of others to do things for them. They were also more extraverted.

The pupils' self-reports as assessed by Cattel's HSPQ Personality Test indicated that there were statistically significant differences on Factors A, F, and H.; Factor A suggests that the victims saw themselves as detached, critical, aloof while the bullies in contrast viewed themselves as more warmhearted, outgoing, easy-going, and participating. Factor F implies that the bullies considered themselves to be more enthusiastic, heedless, happy-go-lucky than the victims who were sober, taciturn and serious. Factor H, moreover, indicated that the bullies were more adventurous, 'thick-skinned' and socially bold. The victims, on the other hand, regarded themselves to be shy, timid and 'threat-sensitive'.

In conclusion, it can be seen that the scientific material on the personal and family characteristics of the bullies and victims from Norway, Sweden, Finland, England and Ireland are broadly similar. Some of the discrepancies in the data within and between countries may reflect methodological differences as well as cultural differences. Future research should attempt to ascertain (1) the extent to which the negative behavioural traits of bullies and victims are causes or effects of the bullying situation in the peer group and (2) examine the relationship that may exist between bullying and a wider anti-social reaction pattern. Also is our bully today, our delinquent tomorrow?

III Preventative and treatment approaches

It is clear that preventative and treatment approaches to bullying are needed. Stability correlations (Olweus, 1979) have indicated the remarkable persistence of aggressive behaviour. Moreover the victims' situation often persists relatively unchanged over many years. Quite apart from relieving, therefore, the humiliation and suffering of victims it is equally important and in the best interest of the perpetrators of bullying that they should not be allowed to continue to behave in this way. West (1973) has, for example, demonstrated by means of a follow-up study of 411 school children that the most significant single factor predictive of later delinquency is troublesomeness at school at age 8. Lewis, (1988), moreover, cites a long-term study undertaken of 800 children in America which revealed that children who bullied in first grade were very likely to grow up into aggressive, anti-social adults. Their marriages were less satisfactory and they were more likely to use violence against their own children. Their personal relationships were poor, they had fewer friends and stood a greater chance of getting into trouble with the law.

Lane (1989) also provides follow-up data of school children which he believes is indicative of a relationship between school bullying and adult violence. For example, a group of 20 pupils labelled as 'impossible' by their teachers were subsequently found to average 15.9 convictions, and 14 of these pupils had convictions for violence. Of particular note is Lane's finding that whereas boys were more likely to develop delinquent careers than girls, those girls who become involved in bullying and delinquency tended to be more delinquent than a comparable group of boys.

In contrast to Scandinavia and Japan, there has been no efforts at national level in the British Isles to prevent or contain bullying in schools. However, there are a few individuals who have taken a special interest in the subject and as a result have made important contributions to our understanding of prevention and treatment approaches to bullying. Lowenstein (1987) for example, in an unpublished manuscript outlined in detail specific treatment measures that he used with two adolescent boys referred to a therapeutic community for severe bullying. He placed particular emphasis on creating an awareness and a conscience within the community concerning the dangers of bullying. Similarly the individual or individuals carrying out the activity of bullying were made aware of how they were affecting others; be it through verbal threats or physical aggression. This was done via individual encounters as well as through group meetings. All members of the community were encouraged to have the confidence to express their feelings about the bullies, knowing their protection was ensured by the staff and the other children. In a group, individuals who were victims of bullying were encouraged to express what had happened and how it affected them emotionally and behaviourally.

In this way, Lowenstein believed three things happened concurrently. Firstly, the victim was able to get rid of his pent up feelings of fear, anxiety, aggression and frustration. Secondly, the bully was made aware of how the victim felt as a human being through his sadistic behaviour. Lowenstein pointed out that bullies on the whole tended to dehumanise their victims. Finally the victim received support from the group while the group condemned the actions of the bully. Lowenstein also emphasised the importance of providing opportunities to behave positively with suitable incentives and rewards if bullying was reduced or indeed in the final analysis ceased altogether. Lowenstein states that 'perhaps one of the greatest difficulties for the two boys was to overcome the intrinsic reinforcement which they received from the bullying of others. Only a combination of punishment for this with positive reinforcement for socialised behaviour could dislodge eventually the gratification from their maladaptive action'. Token economy helped to secure this goal.

The Samaritans have addressed bullying by including the topic in their new educational video package, 'time to talk'. The material is aimed at schools and youth groups. There are teachers' discussion notes and role-playing ideas for classwork. The material does not provide solutions but rather helps children become aware of their own ability to cope and develop coping skills. Titman (1989) has also provided a resource list which should be invaluable in assisting teachers and others involved with children in tackling subjects such as racism and bullying.

Robin Chambers of Stoke Newington School in North London has also attempted to prevent bullying (St. John Brooks, 1985). His school is situated in one of 'the most stressful social services area in the country'. His objective was to undermine the tradition of secrecy. As headteacher of the school he gets all the new children together in the assembly hall and tells them that 'you have the right to come to school without being afraid. This is a "telling school". The rule that you must not tell was invented by bullies, and you will only get trouble if you don't tell'.

Chambers even assured his pupils that they would be protected from reprisals outside school, and was prepared to visit homes over the weekend to make good his promise.

Chambers is very much of the opinion that schools do have the power to control situations. Racist or sexist abuse in the playground is forbidden and sexual stereotyping is discussed in class. Also boys are made to *confront* the whole business 'e.g. what they're trying to do when they swagger'.

Chambers was of the opinion that he was getting somewhere but he was constantly aware of what he called the gap between rhetoric and reality in trying to make such a policy work, and the fact that he was working against the tide. 'If you take your eye off it for two days', he says, 'well, it's like a weed, you keep having to pluck it out, and always will, so long as we've got the kind of society we've got'.

Askew (1989) considers that in order to effect any real change in bullying behaviour, school policies need to be created for a caring ethos and the promotion of such values as respect, caring, tolerance and responsibility for others. Indeed Herbert (1989) goes so far as to propose a whole-curriculum approach to combatting bullying in schools. Pastoral work, he states, is not enough, arguing that the fear and misery induced on victims does not vanish with the end of tutorial time, but is carried on into Maths, Science or Games, not to mention the unsupervised movements between lessons.

Besag (1986) also believes that schools can make a difference to bullying behaviour. She states, 'nothing radical or innovative is required: it is simply a matter of tightening nuts and bolts securely'.

A rather novel approach has been taken by Laslett (1982) who has suggested that setting up a children's court to which pupils can bring complaints against their peers can be one way of reducing bullying in school. Laslett, states he was surprised at the children's sense of justice and their acumen. He quotes an example of a very delicate and very weakly boy who could neither read nor write, and indeed, could hardly walk up the stairs. Yet 'it was striking to see the diminutive child telling children bigger, stronger and more intelligent than he what the court thought of their conduct and he was frequently elected as a Justice because he showed a surprising amount of commonsense'.

In the British Isles strategies tried or comments proposed have predominantly focused on the individual or on the school system. The research data, to date, have highlighted the relationship between disturbed home backgrounds and bullying. Yet parents usually have the most significant influence over children, even in chaotic households. Indeed, there is considerable evidence that working with parents is more effective than direct 'therapy' or intervention with the children. This is, therefore, an important area of future research with regard to bully/victim problems.

The various behavioural systems of linking home and school would be of immediate relevance to teachers. Roland (in this volume) stresses this. It is recognised that many schools have difficulty finding anything by way of rewards and/or punishments which affect the behaviour of disruptive adolescents in school. However, such reinforcers may exist at home. A system, therefore, of recording the child's behaviour at school and reporting this to the parents, who apply reinforcers as appropriate, may serve to get round this difficulty with minimal investment by the school.

Indeed, Topping (1983, 1986) quotes research which has supported significant improvements in behaviour and classroom performance of disruptive adolescents aged up to 19 years with little time investment from the school. Indeed, if one is to be conscious of costs, then according to Topping, parent-training is one of the most cost-effective strategies.

Conclusion

To conclude from this overview, it becomes apparent that there is a need for more detailed and well-controlled research. Both international and cross cultural studies would be particularly important. However, to profit from such studies and to make valid comparisons, the same methodology and terminology should be used. This would avoid to some extent the question marks which hang over the present data on bullying. Namely, whether the differences and inconsistencies in the findings are a product of cultural differences or differences in the descriptions of the children studied. Yates and Smith in this volume make a start on the task.

In working towards a framework of analysis an attempt should be made to develop a comprehensive model which incorporates all the suggested determinants of bullying. Thus, the child, the home, the school and society needs to be examined closely. Furthermore, there should be agreement on the appropriate measurement techniques by which each of the putative factors can be quantified. It is only by such methods that true comparisons of the incidence and types of bullying behaviour can be made.

In time, it should be possible to integrate all the information from the separate levels so that bullying will come to be acknowledged as a multi-factorial phenomenon which can be explained only with reference to the many elements operating at many levels. It is only then that one will be in a position to assess the full range of options for intervention and to implement measures which are most effective.

References

Arora, C. M. and Thompson, D. A. (1987) Defining Bullying for a Secondary School. Education and Child Psychology, 4, (3), 110–120.

Askew, S. (1989) 'Aggressive Behaviour in Boys and to what Extent is it Institutionalised?' in Tattum, D. P. and Lane, D. A. (eds.) Bullying in Schools. Trentham Books, London.

Besag, V. (1986) The Times Educational Supplement, 5th December, 22–23.

Byrne, Brendan, (1987) A Study of the Incidence and Nature of Bullies and Whipping Boys (Victims) in a Dublin City Post-Primary School for Boys. Unpublished M.Ed. Thesis, Trinity College, Dublin.

Darking, L. (1987) Bullying scars the child. The Teacher, Oct. 5.

Department of Education for Northern Ireland (1987) Report of the Working Party on Discipline in Schools in Northen Ireland, HMSO, Belfast.

Frude, N. (1984) 'Frameworks for Analysis' in Frude, N. and Gault, H. (eds.) Disruptive Behaviour in Schools. Wiley, Chichester.

Frude, N. and Gault, H. (eds.) (1984) Disruptive Behaviour in Schools. Wiley, Chichester.

Hargreaves, D. H., Hester, S. K. and Mellor, F. J. (1975) Deviance in Classrooms. Routledge and Kegan Paul, London.

Herbert, G. (1989) A Whole-Curriculum Approach to Bullying in Tattum, D. P. and Lane, D. A. (eds.) Bullying in Schools. Trentham Books, London.

Hillery, B. A. and O'Moore, A. M. (1988) Bullying in the Primary School: A Study of Bully/Victim Problems in Four Dublin City Primary Schools. Submitted for publication.

The Kidscape Primary Kit, Kidscape, 82 Brook Street, London W1Y 1YP.

Lane, D. A. (1989) 'Violent Histories: Bullying and Criminality' in Tattum, D. P. and Lane, D. A. (eds.) Bullying in Schools. Trentham Books, London.

Laslett, R. (1977) 'Disruptive and Violent Pupils: the Facts and the Fallacies'. Educational Review, 29, 152-162.

Laslett, R. (1982) A Children's Court for Bullies. Special Education, 9, 9-11.

Lawrence, J., Steed, D. and Young, P. Disruptive Children (1984), Disruptive Schools? Croom Helm, London.

Lewis, D. (1988) Helping Your Anxious Child. Methuen, London.

Lowenstein, L. F. (1978) 'Who is the Bully?' Bulletin British Psychological Society, 31, 147-149.

Lowenstein, L. F. (1978a) 'The bullied and the non-bullied child'. Bulletin British Psychological Society, 31, 316-318.

Lowenstein, L. F. (1987) 'The Study, Diagnosis and Treatment of Socially Aggressive Behaviour (Bullying) of two Adolescent Boys in a Therapeutic Community'. Unpublished paper.

McNamara, D. (1975) 'Distribution and Incidence of Problem Children in an English County'. Paper presented to British Association for Advancement of Science, Paper, No. 251.

Measor, L. and Woods, P. (1984) Changing Schools: Pupil perspectives on transfer to a secondary school. Open University Press, London.

Mills, W. C. P. (1976) The Seriously Disruptive Behaviour of Pupils in Secondary Schools of one Local Educational Authority. Unpublished M.Ed. Thesis, Birmingham University.

Mitchell, J. and O'Moore (1987) 'The Identification of the problem of bullying in relation to other behaviour problems in the primary school'. Unpublished data.

National Children's Bureau (1977) Violence, Disruption and Vandalism in Schools – a Summary of Research. Highlight No. 32. London.

Newson, J. and E. (1984) 'Parents perspectives on children's behaviour at school', in Frude, N. and Gault, H. (ed.) Disruptive Behaviour in Schools. Wiley, Chichester.

Olweus, D. (1978) 'Aggression in the Schools: Bullies and Whipping Boys'. Hemisphere, Washington, D.C.

Olweus, D. (1979) 'Stability of aggressive reaction patterns in males: a review'. Psychological Bulletin, 84, 852–75.

O'Moore, A. M. (1988) 'Bullying in Schools', Council of Europe Report. DECS/EGT (88) 5 – E, Council for Cultural Co-operation, Strasbourg.

Pringle, M. K. (1973) The Roots of Violence and Vandalism, National Children's Bureau. London.

Proudlock, G. (1985) 'Fighting Back' in Kingfisher Book of Children's Poetry selected by Michael Rosen. Kingfisher, London.

Reid, K. (1984) 'Disruptive behaviour and persistent school absenteeism' in Frude, N., and Gault, H. (ed.) Disruptive Behaviour in Schools. Wiley, Chichester.

Roland, E. (1983) Strategi mot mobbing. Universitetsforlag, Stavanger.

Roland, E. (1989) 'Bullying: The Scandinavian Research Tradition' in Tattum, D. P. and Lane, D. A. (ed.) Bullying in Schools. Trentham Books, London.

Rutter, M. (1967) 'A children's behaviour questionnaire for completion by teachers: preliminary findings'. J. of Child Psychol. and Psychiat., 8, 1–11.

Stephenson, P. and Smith, D. (1987) 'Anatomy of a playground bully'. Education, 18 September, 236–237.

Stephenson, P. and Smith, D. (1989) 'Bullying in the Junior School' in Tattum, D. P. and Lane, D. A. (ed.) Bullying in Schools. Trentham Books, London.

St. John Brooks, C. (1985) 'The School Bullies'. New Society, 6 December, 363–365.

Tattum, D. P. (1982) Disruptive Pupils in Schools and Units. John Wiley, London.

Tattum, D. P. (1989) 'Violence and Aggression in Schools' in Tattum, D. P. and Lane, D. A. (ed.) Bullying in Schools. Trentham Books, London.

Taylor, G. (1987) 'Bullying – Misery for the Child – Heartache for the Parents', Mother Magazine, June.

Titman, W. (1989) Adult Responses to Children's Fears in Tattum, D. P. and Lane, D. A. (eds.) Bullying in Schools. Trentham Books, London.

Topping, K. (1983) Education Systems for Disruptive Adolescents. Croom Helm, London.

Topping, K. (1986) Parents as Educators – Training Parents to Teach Children. Croom Helm, London.

West, D. J. and Farrington, D. P. (1973) Who becomes Delinquent? Heinemann, London.

Wilson, J.R. and Irvine, S.R. (1978) 'Education and Behaviour Problems in Northern Ireland'. Behaviour Disorders, 3, 276–287.

CHAPTER 2

Bullying in Two English Comprehensive Schools

Colin Yates and Peter K. Smith

How serious are bully/victim problems in British schools? It seems that this problem has only begun to be seriously considered. The general problem of discipline in schools was considered recently by the Elton Report (1989), but this focused mainly on difficulties experienced by teachers. What about bullying and victimisation of pupils by each other? Sections 65–67 of the Elton Report did specifically refer to the occurrence of bullying and racial harassment in schools and the need to take action against it. The report refers to the recent publication of 'Bullying in Schools' (Tattum and Lane, 1989) to make the point that bullying may be more extensive than previously thought. Some of the chapters in this book do suggest the problem is very serious. For example, Stephenson and Smith (1989) found that some 23% of children were involved as either bullies or victims, in a survey of teachers in 26 primary schools. Earlier Arora and Thompson (1987) reported that in one small comprehensive school, around 20%–30% of all children between 12 and 14 stated that someone had threatened to hurt them, or had tried to hit them, at least once during the previous week.

These figures seem higher than the kinds of results reported in the extensive Norwegian studies of Olweus (1989). He found that in Norway some 9% of schoolchildren were bullied, and some 7% were bullies, 'now and then' or more frequently. These figures fell to 3% and 2% respectively for 'about once a week' or more frequently. The figures for being bullied (but not for bullying) were less for Norwegian children in junior high school (aged about 13–15 years), falling to about 6% for 'now and then' or more frequently.

It would seem that the British figures for bullies and victims indicate a considerably more prevalent problem than in Norway. However the comparison is not exact because of the different methodologies used. The report by Stephenson and Smith (1989) is based on teachers' reports, while that by Arora and Thompson is based on the 'Life in schools' booklet given to pupils. Olweus by contrast has developed a self-report questionnaire given to pupils, specifically on bully/victim problems, which we have employed with only slight modifications in this study. The present report therefore enables clear and direct comparisons to be made with the extensive Scandinavian findings, albeit with only a limited sample size so far.

The Schools

The study was carried out in two schools, A and B. Both were medium sized comprehensive schools in a large industrial city, with between 600–1000 pupils (School B had 20% less pupils than School A). Both lay on the outskirts of the city, one in the north and one in the south, and had catchment areas which included within their boundaries large council estates which suffered from multiple deprivation. However neither had this problem so much as some of the inner city schools. Both schools were predominantly white (less than 10% of the children were from other ethnic backgrounds) and the children came from mainly working class backgrounds.

The questionnaires were given to the third year (approx. 13 years old) and the fifth year (approx. 15 years old) in each school in February 1989. There were 137 questionnaires from School A (40b, 40g in 3rd year, 29b, 28g in 5th year) and 97 questionnaires from School B (25b, 26g in 3rd year; 25b, 21g in 5th year), giving 234 sets of responses in all. Anonymity and confidentiality were stressed, and it was ensured that pupils did not confer.

The questionnaire closely followed the design of that used by Olweus, but some minor changes were made to suit the British context and current word usage. We asked pupils generally to report on the *last month* at school, this corresponded more or less to the extent of the term so far at the time of assessment. We changed 'last spring' to 'last term', when the former phrase occurred in the original questionnaire. 'Recess time' was charged to 'break time', 'grade' to 'class', and 'student' to 'young person' for these age groups. An additional question about the sex of bullies was added ('who do you think are usually the worst bullies?') and another about any other locations where bullying occurred ('have you been bullied anywhere else in the last month?'). Questions about pupils bullying teachers were omitted. In the questions about whom pupils have told about bullying, we changed 'counsellor' to 'form tutor' and 'mother or father' to 'anyone at home'.

The following definition of bullying was used:

> We say a young person is *being bullied*, or picked on, when another young person, or a group of young people, say nasty and unpleasant things to him or her. It is also bullying when a young person is hit, kicked, threatened, locked inside a room, and things like that. These things may take place frequently and it is difficult for the young person being bullied to defend himself or herself. It is also bullying when a young person is teased repeatedly. But it is *not bullying* when two young people of about the same strength have the odd fight or quarrel.

This is the same definition as used by Olweus with a minor amendment in the last phrase.

The reported frequency of being bullied

The percentage responses to the question 'how often have you been bullied at school?' are shown in Table 1. Overall 22% of pupils reported being bullied 'now and then' or more often, and 10% 'once a week' or more often.

On an analysis of variance by age, sex and school, there were no significant sex or school differences, though there was a significant sex by school interaction. At School A more girls reported being bullied, while at School B more boys reported being bullied, $F(1,226) = 4.3$, $p < .05$. The age difference was nearly significant, $F(1,226) = 3.2$, $p < .08$, with a tendency for younger children to report being bullied more frequently (see Table 1).

When pupils were asked how often thay had been bullied *last term*, the frequencies were 16% for 'now and then' or more often, and 7% for 'once a week' or more often. Of the 51 children who reported being bullied this term, 30 reported being bullied last term as well.

The question 'how often does it happen that other students don't want to spend break time with you and you end up being alone?' assesses what Olweus (1989) calls 'indirect bullying'. The incidence was silimar for boys and girls, being 15% for at least 'now and then' and 3% for 'once a week' or more often.

Table 2.1: Percentage of pupils who reported being bullied at school.

	It hasn't happened	Only once or twice	Now and then	About once a week	About 2 or 3 times a week	About 4 or 5 time a week	Several time a day
Boys (n = 119)	55	24	10	2	5	3	2
Girls (n = 115)	60	17	14	3	2	2	3
3rd yrs (n = 131)	51	24	12	2	5	2	2
5th yrs (n = 103)	65	17	12	2	1	2	2
School A (n = 137)	60	20	10	3	2	2	2
School B (n = 97)	54	22	14	1	5	2	2
Overall	57.3	20.9	12.0	2.1	3.4	2.1	2.1

Where the pupils were bullied

Rather fewer pupils, about 6%, reported being bullied on the way to and from school ('now and then' or more often). Most of these were also bullied at school.

About 18% of pupils reported that they had been bullied somewhere else in the last month. 5% had been bullied in the street where they lived, 4% in town, 3% at a youth club, and 8% elsewhere; a variety of locations were written in here, including on the bus, at the fair (twice), at home (twice), and at the local Chinese take-away shop.

Who bullied them

Two of the questions asked 'in what class is the young person or young people who bully you?' and 'what sex is the young person or young people who bully you?'

In 35% of the cases, the bully was reported to be in the same class as the victim, and in another 31% of cases in a different class in the same year. In 24% of cases the bully was in a class one or more years above, this naturally happening almost only in the third year rather than the fifth year pupils. Only 8% of cases involved a bully from one or more years below, and 2% involved bullies from different years.

Of the boys who reported being bullied, the great majority, 88%, reported being bullied only by boys. This was not the case with girls, 48% of whom reported being bullied by boys, 24% by girls, and 28% by both boys and girls.

The sex difference in who bullies boys and girls is also reflected in the answers to 'who do you usually think are the worst bullies?' (Table 2). Most boys think it is other boys, but many more girls think that boys and girls are both the same ($X^2(3) = 21.1$, $p < .001$).

Table 2.2: Whom pupils report as usually the worst bullies (Percentages, n = 119 boys, 115 girls).

	I don't know	Boys	Girls	Both the same
Boys' replies	14	28	12	46
Girls' replies	19	56	6	19

What form the bullying takes

When asked 'in what way have you been bullied in school?' 64% of the pupils replied they had not been bullied in the last month (a slightly larger proportion than previously, cf. Table 1). Of the remainder, 71% of the replies were that they had 'been teased only'. However 12% were that they had 'been hit and kicked' and 11% that they had 'been both teased, hit and kicked'. Only 2% reported that 'young people demand money or belongings from me.' Rather more girls reported being teased only; rather more boys reported being hit and kicked.

Who knows about the bullying

The pupils were asked if they had told 'any of your teachers or your form tutor' or 'anyone at home' that they had been bullied. Of those pupils who reported being bullied 'now and then' or more frequently, only 15 out of 51 said that they had told their teachers or form tutor about it, and only 21 had told someone at home about it. In answer to a separate question about whether 'any of your teachers' or 'anyone at home' had talked with them about being bullied at school, 13 of these 51 said that a teacher had talked with them once or twice about their being bullied in school; only one pupil reported that the teacher had talked with them several times. Similarly, 17 said that someone at home had talked to them about it once or twice, and 4 more said this had happened several times.

When asked how often 'the teacher' or 'other young people' 'try to put a stop to it when a young person is being bullied at school', teachers were seen as more effective than other pupils, see Table 3. The relatively few pupils who *did* think other young people helped tended to be girls.

Table 2.3: Whom pupils report as trying to put a stop to it when a young person is being bullied (Percentage, n = 234).

	I don't know	Almost never	Once in a while/ Now and then	Often/almost always
Teachers	29	13	20	38
Other young people	24	23	44	9

Feelings of those being bullied

Pupils who were bullied 'now and then' or more frequently were more likely to report being alone at break time (15 out of 51, compared to 20 out of 183 for non-bullied children, $x^2(1) = 9.3$, p<.01). They also more frequently reported being lonely in school 'now and then' or more often (12 out of 51, compared to 18 out of 183 for non-bullied children, $x^2(1) = 5.5$, p<.05), and feeling less well liked than other young people in their class 'now and then' or more often (31 out of 51, compared to 43 out of 183 non-bullied children, $x^2(1) = 23.9$, $p < .001$). However they did not particularly report having fewer friends, or liking break time less.

The reported frequency of bullying

The percentage responses to the question 'how often have you taken part in bullying other young people in school?', are shown in Table 4. Overall 12% of children reported that they bullied other children 'now and then' or more often, and 4% 'once a week' or more often.

On an analysis of variance by age, sex and school, there were no significant age or school effects, or interactions. There was a highly significant sex effect, $F(1,226) = 8.2$, $p < .005$. Only about 5% of girls reported bullying 'now and then' or more often, but 20% of boys did so (see Table 4).

Consistency of reported bullying

When asked about how often they had bullied other young people *last term*, the frequencies were 9% for 'now and then' or more often, and 3% for 'once a week' or more often. Of the 29 children who reported bullying this term, 18 reported bullying last term as well.

Fewer children reported bullying other young people on their way to and from school, about 3% 'now and then' or more frequently. 6 of these 8 children also reported bullying at school.

Who knows about the bullying

Of the 29 self-reported bullies, 20 said that their teacher had *not* talked to them about their bullying other young people; 7 said a teacher had talked to them once or twice, and 2 said this had happened several times. Similarly, 23 of the 29 said that *no-one* at home had talked to them about their bullying other young people; 5 said it had happened once of twice, and one said it had happened several times.

Feelings of bullies

When asked how they usually felt when they saw a young person being bullied in school, 12 of the 29 bullies replied 'I don't feel much' whereas only 23 of the 205 non-bullies did so ($x^2 = 15.8$, $p < .001$). The remaining children chose replies that they thought it 'a bit unpleasant' or 'unpleasant'.

Table 2.4: Percentage of pupils who reported bullying other young people in school.

	It hasn't happened	Only once or twice	Now and then	About once a week	About 2 or 3 times a week	About 4 or 5 time a week	Several time a day
Boys (n = 119)	51	29	13	3	2	0	3
Girls (n = 115)	66	29	3	0	1	0	1
3rd yrs (n = 131)	58	32	5	2	1	0	2
5th yrs (n = 103)	59	25	12	0	2	0	2
School A (n = 137)	62	28	7	1	1	0	2
School B (n = 97)	54	30	10	2	2	0	2
Overall	58.5	29.1	8.1	1.3	1.3	0	1.7

Table 2.5: Number of reports of being bullied in school, and of bullying other young people, in the last month, for boys and girls. (N = 119 boys, 115 girls).

(a) Boys		BULLYING OTHERS			
		It hasn't happened/ only once or twice	Now and then	About once a week or more	
	It hasn't happened/ only once or twice	79	11	4	94
BEING BULLIED	Now and then	8	3	1	12
	About once a week or more	9	1	3	13
		96	15	8	

(b) Girls		BULLYING OTHERS			
		It hasn't happened/ only once or twice	Now and then	About once a week or more	
	It hasn't happened/ ony once or twice	85	3	1	89
BEING BULLIED	Now and then	15	1	0	16
	About once a week or more	9	0	1	10
		109	4	2	

Similarly, 16 of the 29 bullies replied that they would do 'nothing, because it's none of my business', if they saw a young person of their age being bullied in school, compared to only 54 of the 205 non-bullies ($x^2 = 8.7$, $p < .01$). The other children chose replies that they thought they ought to help, or would try to help.

When asked 'what do you think of other young people who bully others?', bullies compared to non-bullies over-reported 'I don't know' (17/29 compared to 70/205) and were similar in 'I can understand why they're doing it' (7/29 compared to 47/205). They under-reported on 'it's hard to understand why they're doing it' (5/29 compared to 74/205) and 'it upsets me a lot that they're doing it' (0/29 compared to 14/205).

Were bullies also victims?

The cross-tabulation of being bullied and of bullying others is shown in Table 5. Of the 51 bullies and 29 victims, 10 were both bullies and victims. Most of these were boys.

Summary of findings

* About 1 pupil in 5 reported being bullied at least 'now and then', and 1 in 10 at least 'once a week', over the last month.
* Boys were almost all bullied by other boys. Girls were bullied more by boys, but considerably by girls as well.
* Most bullies were in the same class or year as the victim.
* The majority of the bullying took the form of teasing but about a quarter involved physical violence.
* These victims of bullying were more likely to be alone at break time and to feel lonely and less well liked at least now and then.
* Less then half of these pupils had talked to a teacher, or anyone at home about their being bullied. This was despite a *general* perception by many pupils that teachers would try to stop bullying. Not many felt other pupils would do so.
* About 1 pupil in 8 reported bullying other young people at least 'now and then', and about 1 in 25 reported doing so at least 'once a week'.
* Boys are about four times more likely than girls to report bullying others, and for boys the previous figures rise to 1 in 5, and 1 in 12, respectively.
* Over two-thirds of the bullies reported that no-one had talked to them about their bullying, at school or at home.
* Bullies were generally more tolerant of bullying in others, than non-bullies were.

Comparison with previous findings

These findings are broadly consistent with the Scandinavian research concerning the context of bullying, but differ considerably in the overall frequency of bully/victim problems, which appear to be at least *twice* those typically reported in Norway.

As regards the context of the bullying, the age and sex trends parallel those shown in other studies. Olweus (1989) has reported a decrease in age with frequency of being bullied, but not in frequency of bullying; and a predominant sex difference in the latter. Similarly, the Norwegian studies have found that in junior high school less than half of the students involved have talked to teachers or parents about bully/victim problems.

Like Olweus (1989), we found that bullying on the way to and from school was considerably less frequent than bullying at school. Olweus (1989) concluded from this that 'the school is, no doubt, where most of the bullying occurs'. However we did include an extra question on whether pupils had been bullied anywhere else, and nearly as many pupils responded to this as replied that they had been bullied in school at least 'now and then'. Of course, this extra question tapped a large number of places where bullying might happen. Thus, it probably is true that the school is the one place where bullying is most likely, as Olweus suggests; but it also seems that in aggregate, a roughly equal amount of bullying may happen outside school.

In general, the consistency of these findings with those reported in Scandinavia is impressive. However in one respect our findings are markedly discrepant. This is in the overall incidence of bully/victim problems.

If we take at least 'now and then' as the criterion, our incidence figures for being a victim are 22%, and for bullies, 12%. This compares with figures from Olweus (1989) of about 6% and 7%, respectively, at this age level. If we take at least 'once a week' as the criterion, our incidence figures for being a victim are 10%, and for bullies, 4%. This compares with figures from Olweus (1989) of about 3%, and 2%, respectively, for all ages. Using this same criterion Roland (1989) reports an incidence of about 1-3% for being bullied, and 1-3% for bullies, for 13 to 15 year olds in S-W Norway.

Thus our present figures are about three times larger for victims, and twice as large for bullies, than the Norwegian data, independent of the criteria taken.

There could be a number of explanations for this. Firstly, of course, this data is only obtained from 2 schools. Perhaps these schools are exceptionally troubled by this problem. However we believe them to be not untypical of large city comprehensive schools in Britain. They were not selected on the basis of any particular problems being reported. Other studies we are carrying out in middle and secondary schools also seem to be finding a comparable level of bully/victim problems. This level is also broadly consistent with that reported by Stephenson and Smith (1979) on the basis of teacher report (23% involved in bully/victim problems in junior school) and to that reported by Arora and Thompson (1987) on the basis of 12-14 year old pupils reply to the 'Life in schools' booklet, at a small comprehensive school.

Secondly, one might question the validity of questionnaire responses. However, while it is always possible that a few pupils may fake answers to the questionnaire, we have generally been impressed by the seriousness with which pupils treat it. The responses to the questionnaire are consistent, both within the questionnaire when responses are compared (for example when the incidence of being bullied is compared across a number of questions which assess this, directly or indirectly), and in the structure of the answers compared to other available data. We are currently comparing questionnaire and interview data on bully/victim problems; our provisional conclusion so far is that the questionnaire is preferable to the interview as a confidential, anonymous means of getting information on bullying.

In summary, this and other evidence is beginning to suggest quite strongly that bully/victim problems in British schools are considerable, and markedly greater in extent than in Norwegian schools. We also know that victims experience less happy and at times very distressing circumstances with peers, while bullies are experiencing a training in aggressive behaviour which may well potentiate future antisocial activities. If bullying and victimisation are at anything like the levels reported, there is no excuse for complacency in our response. A coordinated intervention strategy has been shown to be effective in the Norwegian context (Olweus, 1989). It is urgent that in Britain too, we not only find out more about the nature of the problem, but also take active steps to remedy it.

References

Arora, C. M. J. and Thompson, D. A. (1987) Defining bullying for a secondary school. *Education and Child Psychology*, **4**, 110-120.

Elton Report (1989) Discipline in Schools. London: HMSO.

Olweus, D. (1989) Bully/victim problems among schoolchildren: basic facts and effects of a school based intervention program. In K. Rubin and D. Pepler (eds.) *The development and treatment of childhood aggression*. Hillsdale, N. J. Erlbaum.

Roland, E. (1989) Bullying: the Scandinavian research tradition. In D. P. Tattum and D. A. Lane (eds.) *Bullying in Schools*. Stoke-on-Trent, Trentham Books.

Stephenson, P. and Smith, D. (1989) Bullying in the junior school. In D. P. Tattum and D. A. Lane (eds.), *Bullying in Schools*, Stoke-on-Trent, Trentham Books.

Tattum, D. P. and Lane, D. A. (1989) *Bullying in Schools*. Stoke-on-Trent, Trentham Books.

CHAPTER 3

Violence, Bullying and Counselling in the Iberian Peninsula.

Maria Manuel Vieira da Fonseca, Isabel Fernandez Garcia and Gumersindo Quevedo Pérez.

Introduction

Max Weber has stated that knowledge only arises as such when it becomes relevant for the scientific community: '. . . only valuable ideas, prevailing over the investigator and his time, will establish the object of study and its limits.' (Weber, 1977).

In the field of Social and Human Sciences, particularly after World War II, one has witnessed a transfer from the *public sphere* to the *private sphere*.

Subjects and areas traditionally considered as marginal, or unworthy of either rational or scientific analysis, now deserve special attention. Family, private life, leisure as well as outside culture, economy and behaviour, are themes which receive attention in the market place of scientific research.

Such an attitude obviously points to a new perspective (See Ariès, 1973 and Badinter, 1980), which gives rise to the proliferation of studies on themes like informal authority in school, communication proportions, 'juvenile culture', group dynamics and insubordination, violence and delinquency.

It is precisely in the context of this new awareness that the bullying problem in school becomes apparent. A few years ago adults used to consider it an underground phenomenon, particularly involving children and young people. Nowadays, it receives the attention of investigators and educators. However, it is so recent as a subject of research that one scarcely finds theoretical works on it, in spite of the apparent permanence of the problem.

If one accepts the Scandinavian definition; 'longstanding violence, mental or physical, conducted by an individual or a group and directed against an individual who is not able to defend himself in the actual situation', bullying is then a rather important and intricate problem.

This concept transcends a great number of situations, involving different types of participants; it has no defined limits since it can involve anything from the exclusion, dismissal, repudiation of a schoolfriend to systematic aggression involving threats, permanent intimidation, everyday humiliation, blackmail and extortion.

We can consider bullying as a chess game, played on different boards, with its roots in very diversified fields, e.g. the school itself, psychology, sociology, politics, economy and even anthropology.

Such a frame deserves an interactive approach in order to achieve a better understanding. However, understanding will not be achieved without articulation of the cultural specificity of each country and, most particularly, of each educational system. This may produce original explanations of the factors which shape the expression of the phenomenon.

In this chapter on the bullying problem in Portugal and Spain, we shall suggest the need for such a multidisciplinary and multicultural approach. We shall attempt to define the problem, along with social and educational issues relative to each country.

Portugal, Maria Manuel Vieira de Fonseca

One can say that, in Portugal, the bullying problem is not yet scientifically perceptible. We do not know of any specific references; it can be found scattered in news or articles on juvenile aggressiveness, misappropriate behaviour or violence in school. This last exception, i.e. violence within the school context, will enable us to present a few considerations about bullying in Portugal. However, it will be necessary first to provide a brief overview of the present Portuguese educational system and, its social context.

A 'dualistic society in development' (Nunes, 1964)

Portuguese society is crossed by strong contrasts between vast areas where traditional activities are quite important and, on the other hand, modernity pivots which, although in expansion, is still very circumscribed.

Figure 3.1: The Portuguese Educational System

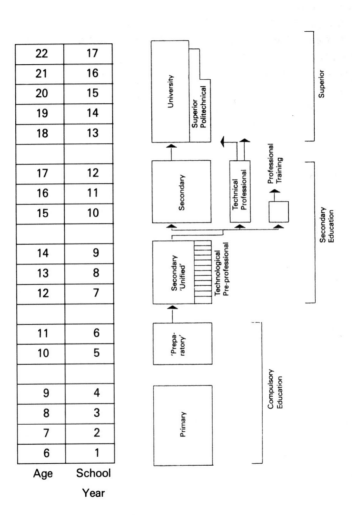

Age	School Year
22	17
21	16
20	15
19	14
18	13
17	12
16	11
15	10
14	9
13	8
12	7
11	6
10	5
9	4
8	3
7	2
6	1

Such a disparity is expressed by social stratification, (I.N.E. 1983), and lower educational levels in Portuguese society. For example, in 1982, around 19% of the Portuguese people older than 14 were illiterate, 12% could read and write but had no certification and 42% had only attended the first 4 years of primary school. The remaining 27% had followed to higher levels.

Compulsory education in Portugal only consists of six years, from the age of 6 up to 11 years of age.

From figure 3.1 (page 37) we shall get a global picture of the Portuguese educational system:

Some characteristics of the system must be pointed out as they can be responsible for the development of bullying and violence at school:

1. The enormous quest for secondary education in the last two decades has gone far beyond the capacity of the existing schools, mainly in the urban and suburban areas, causing an excessive concentration of pupils, even when organised in turns, reaching 3,000 students at certain schools.
2. The school course of each student requries constant changes and adaptations to new environments since he will attend three different schools: after four years at a primary school he will be transferred to a preparatory school for two years, having a specialized teacher for each subject, and finally he will be transferred to yet another school to attend the secondary course.
3. The fairly high rates of repetition, 15–25%, (Fonseca et al., 1987) that occur at primary school, preparatory and the first three years of secondary are responsible for the heterogeneity of age in the classes, this possibly being in itself a propitiating agent of the bullying phenomenon, mainly at levels attended by adolescents – no doubt a very critical age.
4. It is well known that a school is also a 'community of young people' included in an educational institute which, for such a reason, establishes a 'plentiful sphere of social comparison' (Piolat, 1986). Since the classes are heterogeneous, certain differences either physical (age) or intellectual ones (most of all those of the school itself, by evaluating the pupils as 'apto' or 'nao apto') assume large proportions, decisively marking the pupils' behaviour.

Confrontations at school

In trying to find out the meaning of the evolution and patterns of violence at school, we have examined the news on this subject that was published in seven different Lisbon newspapers from April 1974 up to December 1986.

The first of these dates was chosen because the April Revolution had restored the civil rights and the freedom of the press in Portugal.

Such a proceeding has its own limits since one can only find the news generally accepted as notorious enough to be published instead of a thorough view of the events that actually took place. Nevertheless, we consider that it is important to the knowledge of the phenomenon of violence.

The analysis clearly indicates two periods with different kinds of violence:

1974-1978	1978-1986
FIGHTS and POLITICAL PROSECUTION	a) VANDALISM and BURGLARY of SCHOOLS b) BURGLARY of school STAFF and PUPILS.
Those involved:	Those involved:
STUDENTS	PUPILS

Between 1974 and 1978 – a time of stress for the Portuguese society – we find twelve news items concerning violence, all of them related to fights and political persecutions among the students.

These confrontations occur mostly in the two largest towns; Lisbon and Oporto, and in their outskirts. The students' political beliefs seem to be the cause of most of the violent actions taking place at schools.

From 1978 to 1986 a progressive political appeasement changed the patterns of violence.

We have found 25 references to actions that can be divided into two different kinds: on the one hand, vandalism and burglary against the schools with the sole purpose of destroying the premises, and on the other hand, burglary during the day time of school staff and pupils mainly.

Secondary schools and also preparatory or even primary schools are the chosen targets of these two kinds of violence led by groups of young people or youngsters (pupils or not), establishing a constant state of alarm.

Some of these news reports result from the frequency of assaults against the same school and are particularly apparent in peripheral zones, in overcrowded, precarious and unsafe buildings attended by pupils from lower socioeconomic groups.

Young people living in the modern characterless peripheral areas of crowded towns; with no recognizable culture – in contradiction to the old communities – develop 'chronic, disorganized behaviour' expressed in a violence which is dangerous for its unpredictable character (Dubet, 1987).

However, violent expressions against school as an institution seem to mean that many young Portuguese do not consider it a place where they feel like staying. The effect of school context on pupils' behaviour appears in a system (or school) that favours success and competition instead of other broader purposes. This may influence those who fail towards misbehaviour (Figueira–Macdonough, 1986).

The recent restrictions on university admission, the absence of intermediate technical studies and the need for improved employment perspectives for the graduates of the secondary level who have traditionally been much undervalued in the market, will probably have generated increasing competition. If one links such circumstances to an excessive concern with academic success, one will understand the above mentioned situations of conflict.

Pupils' views on violence

The methodology we developed in order to obtain pupils' views on violence at school was based on pupils' essays.

In a Secondary school on the outskirts of Lisbon, pupils of the 7th and 9th forms (12 and 14 years of age) were told to write on the general theme of 'Violence at School'. Thus we obtained a description of what they perceived as violent behaviour.

The analysis of the essays revealed no significant differences between the two age groups. Both point to the same expressions of violence and these can be divided into three categories:

1. School violence (as an institution) against pupils:

In the majority of the cases this includes references to aggressiveness:

a. *from the teacher*: (the most frequent): '. . . bored teachers use pupils as scapegoats', '. . . when pupils are sent out of the classroom having done no harm', '. . . when teachers do not respect their pupils', '. . . when teachers show off their superiority'.

b. *from the institution, lato senso*: '. . . forbid pupils to leave school during breaks'.

2. Pupil violence against the institution:

Disrespectful attitudes towards attendants and teachers, destruction of premises and school material, making trouble inside the classrooms.

3. Pupils against pupils:

Sometimes, such violence is abstractly described with no reference to the aggressor, the victims or the explicit consequences: '... fighting to keep his territory' (7th form), '... quarrels between pupils' (9th form).

Violent situations may be seen as coincidental with bullying: '... the oldest hit the young ones, for no reason, just to show off' (7th form), '... a way of showing you are stronger and more powerful, pretending to be better than the others' (9th form), '... supplying drugs to innocent pupils, and if they refuse, they compel them to accept, even using emotional blackmail', '... big shots do whatever they like and try to give orders even to their own superiors', '... when a 16 year old boy humiliates the smaller ones' (9th form), '... rejecting one of the school-mates, mainly if he doesn't do anything' (9th form), '... take things away from other fellows' (9th form).

'Pupils against pupils' was the most frequent expression used in the essays. We do think such experiences are shared by many other pupils in other schools. Bullying does exist in Portugal. These statements also clearly reveal a kind of psychological violence – a certain relation between pupil and teacher that doesn't often appear in bullying studies, although it fits within a definition of bullying.

Spain, Isabel Fernandez Garcia and Gumersindo Quevedo Pérez

The Spanish educational system can – like the Portuguese – be characterized by the great process of change undergone during the last decade, due partially to the social change which both countries have experienced. The Spanish New Law of Education (LODE 1985) established the grounds for a new approach where the different sectors of the educational community (teachers, parents, students as well as local administration) all became supervisors of the various activities undertaken within the school. This has brought together traditionally separate areas such as finance, teaching methods, curricula, social interaction, etc.

Attendance at a specific school based on proximity to home transformed the schools. This, together with a vast majority of the teachers being in their 30's (especially in the public sector) has created an educational panorama filled with ideas and experimentation which quite often comes out more like an outburst of enthusiasm than as any rational, planned program.

However, efforts have been made to rationalize and channel these new trends. The future (1992) renewal of the secondary schools' curriculum (La Reforma), which has been tested in different schools all over the country for the last five years, hopes to solve some of the deficiencies which early specialization creates.

Education is now compulsory up to the EGB (Educación General Básica) primary-intermediate level which concludes at the approximate age of 14. This is studied at one single school where even the kindergarten level (ages 4 or 5) has also been completed. The EGB thus starts at the age of 6. It is then divided into three cycles: 1–2, 3–4–5, and 6–7–8. This is illustrated in the figure below:

Figure 3.2: The Spanish School System

(SECONDARY EDUCATION IS OPTIONAL)

AGE	GRADE	CYCLE	
13 12 11	8 7 6	3 3 3	
10 9 8	5 4 3	2 2 2	COMPULSORY
7 6	2 1	1 1	
5 4	Kindergarten		OPTIONAL

The first two cycles are taught by one single teacher except for Physical Education and Religion or Ethics. At public schools the same teacher tends to stay with a class-group for the entire cycle.

The third cycle, and usually the most difficult one, requires different teachers for different subjects. Each class has a teacher–tutor in charge.

Of the EGB schools 60% are public and most of them do not exceed 600 students in total. Class numbers range from 25 to 40 students, depending on the age and the area in which the school is located. The lower grades tend to have fewer in each class as the demographic rate is decreasing considerably. However, the private schools – mainly Roman Catholic – quite often hold 1000 or more students with an average of 35–40 per class. The choice of which school a child should attend depends on the parents and it is not necessarily an economic decision, as up to the end of the EGB, most of the private branch is subsidized by the state through agreements between the Schools and the Ministry of Education, making it accessible to a large number of the population.

Major infrastructure development at the EGB level has already been achieved. There are enough buildings and equipment as well as a satisfactory teacher–student rate. However, more sophisticated problems are flourishing: such as the integration of disabled students, the need for psychological and pedagogic teams to participate actively both with teachers and students, the adjustment of curricula to fit our social and human needs, the development of more practical subjects, etc.

Social interaction is mainly dealt with through extra-curricular activities (visits to museums, factories, theatres, etc.). Here the parents' association plays a major role as it frequently finances and organizes these activities. Thus social problems such as delinquency, violence, drug abuse, lack of sexual education, etc. are shadows which are not frequently faced up to nor exposed in the open, but rather tend to come out only under special circumstances.

Violence within the school grounds has passed through different stages, from stealing school equipment (this is however slowly decreasing due to the introduction of alarm systems, barred windows and watch dogs), to teacher–student aggression and vice versa which in the last two years has become quite a newsworthy issue. No major attention has been given to gang violence which is quite common particularly in the outskirts of big cities.

Bullying in Spain: A first study

Bullying is often identified as 'growing up' or simply a fact of life. There is a problem in defining it. However, once it is understood most people end up snapping their fingers and describing countless cases where 'that' happened.

No serious articles nor studies have yet been undertaken in this field although there is quite a large amount of literature on conflict-solving, commonly referring to deviant behaviour, academic failure or poor relationship dynamics between subgroups or individuals within a class.

The following study on bullying which we will present briefly here, was conducted through a multiple choice questionnaire presented to 1,200 students in the area of Madrid. Thus it is not representative of rural or small-town Spain. It was presented in three different areas of Madrid:

(a) RETIRO   (b) USERA-VILLAVERDE   (c) PARLA

The diagram opposite shows the main characteristics of the schools that participated:
As we can see, a total of 10 schools participated in our survey.

The Retiro area represents middle and upper-middle class. Most inhabitants are professionals or civil servants. In the Usera-Villaverde region which comprises both town centre and outskirts of Madrid, it is predominantly middle and lower middle class where employment is mostly concentrated on skilled workers and service occupations. About 25 km away from Madrid, we find the region of Parla, a dormitory town. Here we find mostly manual workers, some construction and some farming. The outer right-hand column shows the average of pupils per class. This shows that an average of 40 is not uncommon but that this number does vary according to the size of the school.

The questionnaire defined bullying as *repetitive violence, both physical and mental, executed by an indiviudal or group towards a subject who is not capable of defending himself in such a situation and who hence becomes a victim.* In some schools the questionnaire was handed out by a teacher while in others by a member of the 'study group' who explained it and went through it with the different classes. We were basically looking for general information about the following:

(a)   Do students fear school, grades, other children, etc?
(b)   Does bullying take place?
(c)   How does bullying manifest itself?
(d)   When and where does it happen?
(e)   How do they react to bullying, both personally and as a passive on-looker?

Total results

Figure 3.3 shows the total results on 12 questions concerning bullying. More questions were asked than those considered here, but we chose to leave them out as they are not essential for the understanding of bullying.

It is obvious that bullying does take place with nearly a fifth of the school population. Although the bullying situation was immediately recognized, whether they themselves were actual bullies was harder to acknowledge. We see, however, that 17.3% do consciously admit to bullying others.

REGION	LOCATION CLASS	NO. OF SCHOOLS	TYPE	NO. OF STUDENTS	GRADES	SIZE CLASS
RETIRO	centre middle- high class prof./civil servants	4	1-pb 1-pv 1-pl 2-RC	600 1000 1000 1000	3-5-7	30-35 40 40
USERA-	centre- outskirts	4	2-pb	400	5-7	25-30
VILLA VERDE	middle-low skilled. Service work		2-pv	1000	3-5-7	40
PARLA	dormitory town manual work construct. agriculture	2	2-pb	600	3-5-7	35-40

key: pb = public school pv = private school RC = Roman Catholic pl = progressive liberal

Figure 3.3: Total results from bullying – questionnaire.

QUESTION	PERCENTAGE
Fear of other children	14.5
Bullied this term	17.2
Physical aggression	12.7
Laughed at/mocked	19.3
Hidden material/theft	13.9
Isolated/rejected	7.2
Recess	42.1
During class	20.2
I don't do anything	23.3
I tell (parents/friends/teacher)	38.7
I go against my aggressor	37.8
I bully others	17.3

Physical and verbal bullying is the most frequent. Theft and the hiding of objects is next, which can be perfectly understood as they are two of the most important issues in a school's daily life and are usually considered as isolated cases and rarely explained through bullying. Third is physical aggression while the least common form, by a large margin, is 'rejection'.

Break time is the main period for bullying, however class periods are important, which correlates with the fact that most bullying takes place in the form of mocking, being laughed at etc.

When asked about their reactions towards being bullied, the figures show that most of the children tend to do something about it, although 23.3% do not do anything.

Girls and boys

In the table below it does however, become apparent that boys and girls react differently. Here we can see that girls tend to be much more communicative, mainly with their teachers and parents. On the other hand, we see that the boys tend to be more aggressive; 42.7% of the boys say they would go against their aggressor, whereas 29.2% of the girls say they would.

There is no major difference between boys and girls as concerns the question on whether the bullying takes a form of rejection. 7.3% of the girls say they are rejected, and 7.1% of the boys report on this.

We see that more boys (16%) than girls (12.3%) report on being afraid of other children, whereas more girls (19.6%) than boys (16%) report on

Figure 3.4 Girls' and boys' answers shown in percentages:

QUESTION	GIRLS	BOYS
Fear of other children	12.3	16
Bullied this term	19.6	16
Physical aggression	9.2	14.4
Laughed at/mocked	19.9	19
Hidden material/theft	12	14.9
Isolated/rejected	7.3	7.1
Recess	42.8	41.9
During class	24.2	18.5
I don't do anything	21	24.6
I tell (parents/friends/teacher)	49.6	32.5
I go against my aggressor	29.2	42.7
I bully others	15.5	18

being bullied this term. Perhaps an explanation to this lies in the next question and its answers from both sexes. Here we see that physical violence is more apparent among boys than among girls, and it might be this the boys have reported on.

Public and private schools

Figure 3.5 Results from public and private schools shown in percentages:

QUESTION	PRIVATE	PUBLIC
Fear of other children	15.8	12.6
Bullied this term	17.9	17
Physical aggression	14.2	10.3
Laughed at/mocked	19.5	19.9
Hidden material/theft	16.8	9.4
Isolated/rejected	6.3	8.5
Recess	41.3	43.6
During class	19.7	21
I don't do anything	22.1	25.9
I tell (parents/friends/teacher)	36.8	42.7
I go against my aggressor	40.8	31.2
I bully others	14	21

As we can see from the above table, there are few major differences between public and private schools. It is however evident that stealing and hiding the possessions of others is considered more of a problem at the private schools involved (16.8%) than at the public schools (9.4%).

Another difference is that whereas most pupils at the private schools would go against their aggressors, the public school pupils would prefer to tell their teachers, parents, friends about the bullying taking place. Yet this is not sufficient evidence to maintain that private school pupils are more aggressive than public school pupils. Further studies would be needed in which one also considers other aspects of the school environment which can influence the outcome.

Age

Figure 3.6: Results according to age shown in percentages:

QUESTION	3RD	5TH	7TH
Fear of other children	15.3	10.8	17.3
Bullied this term	21	18.4	12.4
Physical aggression	14.4	11.3	13.5
Laughed at/mocked	18.7	16.5	22.7
Hidden material/theft	19.3	13.8	7
Isolated/rejected	9.8	7.7	5.4
Recess	47.7	39.1	38.1
During class	17.6	20.4	22.1
I don't do anything	22.1	22.6	22.8
I tell (parents/friends/teacher)	39.8	30.5	32.5
I go against my aggressor	38	46.6	44.5
I bully others	16	23.9	12.2

The youngest are bullied the most, and the figure decreases with age. This is in accordance with other Scandinavian findings as well. However, the highest rate for fearing other children, grades and teachers was among the oldest children. The youngest have to be careful about their belongings as stealing and hiding other children's belongings rates highest among this age group.

Recess is the worst time for the youngest as here they are bullied the most, while for seventh graders it is the class period which becomes the worst as fear of grades and teachers increases considerably at this age.

Fifth grade shows a lowering in the curve for most variables, except in actually being a bully. It is the terminal year of the cycle when they begin to hold a certain status compared with the youngest.

New trends and approaches in conflict solving: the tutoring system

Tutoring is becoming a major issue both at EGB and Secondary Education level. The tutor–teacher is required to become an expert in handling social, human and academic problems. This is not only imposed and promoted by the administration in the way of scheduling special tutoring periods, but also by an increasing number of watchful parents who are slowly taking an active role in their children's education. However, the tutor will not have received qualified training to face the academic nor the human situations, and quite often attains the skills required in such cases only through practical experience.

Most EGB schools in the public sector receive the visit of the so-called 'psycho-pedagogic teams' which belong to the Administration and collaborate with the teachers from a specific geographic area. These teams are helpful for specific students who are considered borderline cases with learning difficulties. Needless to say, the real pulse of the dynamic process of each class group relies heavily on the team of teachers that know the group, if that is the case, or more specifically on the tutor in charge of them.

This tutor is a basic element, and it is the case that a tutor who is trusted, liked and respected by the majority of the class can be the keystone for the improvement of the group both in terms of self-esteem and academic achievements. The tutor is always a teacher who knows the group, both as a teacher inside the class as well as outside it through organizing activities and trips, meeting the parents, counselling, attending to personal problems, etc. The tutor acts as the link between the students and the teachers while at the same time also having to deal with academic problems.

When solving any kind of conflict, the tutor is the expert who should have all the available information as well as the capacity to judge the situation in an objective manner. When a conflict gets out of hand, it is ultimately raised to the 'Jefe de Estudios' who in such cases should take special disciplinary measures. If the case is extreme, it goes to the school council (formed by teachers, parents and students) which then decides and passes judgement according to the school rules.

On taking a closer look at the tutoring process, we observe that most cases of conflict rarely go beyond the tutor level, while the furthest they reach is the Jefe de Estudios level.

The educational trend in cases of conflict is that of *prevention rather than discipline*. Prevention, and if necessary, intervention, can be summarized in the following models:

Prevention

(1)   *Receiving information.*

(a) *Knowing* the student as an individual. Through questionnaires, informal talks with parents, passive observation, different types of reports, etc.

(b) *Finding out* the different groups within the class. Knowing how they relate to each other and what status they hold within the class as a whole, sociograms, passive observation, etc.

(c) *Being aware* of the school rules, its limits and demands.

(2) *Channelling information*

(a) *Helping to develop self-esteem.* This can be simply defined by 'creating a positive attitude towards the work, behaviour and hopes the students have. Introducing competition and comparisons with others as a game and never as an end in itself.'

(b) *Opening means of communication.* The creation of a dialogue within the class, giving them the chance to express not only their knowledge but also their controlled feelings, worries and expectations. It can be the keystone to understanding and hence to channelling actual or future problems.

(c) *Motivating participation.* Neither of the above two sections can happen if the students do not feel that they are acting their own play. All this, plus learning to work together, to collaborate and to get to know each other, is the nucleus for positive social interaction.

Despite the prevention phase, conflict does occur. The following are some steps that can be taken when intervening:

Intervention

(a) *Detecting the problem.* Teachers and parents are quite often blind to the obvious. Very often a problem is not such until we label it. With bullying, this first step is one often not taken.

(b) *Facing/accepting the problem.* Once a conflict is recognized as such, the next step is to decide what to do about it. Sometimes it is better to wait and to intervene at the right time, but quite often this is a difficult step. It is the role of the tutor to light the spark by talking about the case to the people involved either making it public or keeping it personal. Usually this step is not reached in bullying problems. It has not been identified as a problem and neither the bully-victim nor the teacher–parents wish to openly admit it. There is a sense of weakness, and marginality which makes it a touchy situation. Most often it is ignored and it is hoped that it will work itself out.

(c) *Reach an agreement.* Once a conflict has been analyzed, then an agreement which implies certain changes in behaviour should be reached. This takes for granted that the people involved in the conflict all know the new pact.

(d) *The agreement is maintained and supervised.* If broken, new and more serious agreements have to be reached. If this does not work the disciplinary chain through to councelling should be set in motion.

Summary

It can be argued that although the Portuguese and Spanish educational systems have become more open and are trying to develop the model of the 'educational community' with the participation of the different sectors, there are still major human-social problems which are not given enough attention. This is true in the case of bullying which is often understood as a non-problem or as isolated events. The Portuguese investigation into newspaper articles and the study involving pupils' own views on violence in school, show that bullying is evidently apparent in the Portuguese society. The Spanish questionnaire study shows that bullying takes place most frequently in the form of psychological bullying and secondly by way of stealing and theft. The youngest third graders account for the highest percentages of victims, while the fifth graders account for the highest number of bullies.

The tutoring system has been concerned with academic achievement, discipline and counselling. One has not yet started to detect concern with the bullying phenomenon and thus it stays in the background.

References

Anuario Estatistico, I.N.E. 1983.

Aries, P., 1973 *Lénfant et la vie familiale sous l'Ancien Regime.* Ed. du Seuil, Paris.

Badinter, E., 1980 *Lámour en plus.* Flammarion, Paris.

Dubet, F., 1987 *Conduites marginales des jeunes et classes sociales.* 'Revue Francaise de Sociologie', Paris, XXVIII.

Figueira-McDonough, J., 1986 *School context, gender and delinquency.* 'Journal of Youth and Adolescence' New York, vol. 15, no. 1.

Fonseca, M., Nunes, M., Claudino, G., Bouattour, S. 1987 *Education et emploi des femme au Portugal – une évolution contrastée.* Institut International de Planification de l'Education, UNESCO.

Nunes, S., 1964 *Portugal, sociedade dualista em evolucao.* 'Análise Social', Lisboa, vol. II, no. 7-8.

Piolat, M., 1986 *Identidade e experiencia escolar no início do ensino secundário.* 'Análise Psicológica', Lisboa, 1(V).

Weber, Max, 1977 *Sobre a teoria das ciencias sociais.* Ed. Presenca, Lisboa.

Portuguese newspapers consulted:
'Expresso', 'Diário de Notícias', 'Jornal da Educacao', 'Correio da Manha', 'O Diário', 'A Capital', 'O Dia'.

All statistics referring to the survey carried out in Spain have been calculated and supplied by Almudeno Rebollo of the Asociacion de Diplomados en Estadística, Madrid.

CHAPTER 4

Bullying in the Dutch School System

Niek de Kruif

Diversity in the Dutch society

If you want to understand the bullying problem in Holland, you need to know about our history. Holland has been a colonial monarchy for several centuries; the Dutch conquered South Africa, Indonesia (the Dutch Indies), they even possessed New York for quite some time. Surinam was Dutch, and even now, in the eighties, we still rule over seven small islands off the coast of South America (the Netherlands Antilles).

The Dutch people are a mixture of Europeans and people from the colonies who chose to migrate to Holland because the standard of living is higher here. When most of our colonies became independent, lots of Indonesians and people from Surinam and the Netherlands Antilles came to Europe to stay. Most of these immigrants came in the sixties and seventies. Also in the seventies, our country invited thousands of workers from Turkey, Spain and Morocco to settle in Holland and do the menial work which the Dutch chose not to do.

This decade there is a lot of unemployment in Holland. Its first victims were those who came from other areas of the world. The families that became the victims of our economic problems mostly have a large number of children to feed. These children often have problems with the Dutch language and with the Dutch way of life.

Beside the cultural diversity of our country, Holland is the most densely populated country in the world (even higher than Japan or China). So, on a very small piece of land, we have a large number of people representing several cultural backgrounds. In the big cities like Amsterdam, Rotterdam and The Hague, it is no exception to find schools with only 10% Dutch children. Even in the small town where I work there is a school where 50% of the children are Turkish.

In addition to our 'ethnic story', we also have the story of the Dutch tolerance. For centuries Holland has provided shelter for all who were persecuted in their own countries. French protestants in the time of Louis XIV, the Huegenots, Jews from all over Europe found a new home in Holland. Even now, in the eighties, refugees find a home in Holland.

I think that because we have this historical background, people in Holland have a rather extreme sense of justice and tolerance. For instance, South Africa was once Dutch (apartheid is a Dutch word!) and we are, because of that, rather aggressive towards that system. Organizations like Amnesty International and Green Peace have many supporters here.

Our school system is a mirror of our history. We feel very responsible for the people of our former colonies and take great pains to ensure integration of, for example, the Turkish and Maroccan people. For example, the Turkish pupils at my school (9 pupils in all) get OETC-education. This means that they get lessons in their own language and culture from a Turkish teacher for half a day every week. Integration is working slowly but securely to overcome racial problems.

Bullying in the Dutch society

As a result of the specific measures taken, the cause of violence in the Dutch schools is not primarily racial.

Violence is mostly a problem in the big cities and in families suffering stresses. Because our school system is also rather tolerant, we have not yet developed specific means to cope with these problems.

Primary school classes in Holland tend to be rather large. It is no exception to have more than 35 pupils in one classroom, and often they are two classes combined. Last year one of my teachers had a 1/2-form with 38 children on her own. You will understand that it was impossible for that teacher to see everything that went on in her class or to give good education. A bullying problem can easily be hidden in large classes.

Bullying is a topic which has not been investigated very much in the Netherlands. Only recently has interest on the topic been raised. In February 1988 Bob van der Meer published his book 'De zondebok in de klas' (The scapegoat in the class) which is one of the first attempts at recognizing this problem. Bob van der Meer is as teacher of Physical Education and a psychologist. His book is based on a ten-year study of his own pupils. In this study, the author defines 'scapegoat' as:

'The scapegoat-phenomenon is the hostile and aggressive action towards an innocent and helpless victim, when there is no clear frustration, cause or when there is no reason to attack somebody.' (van der Meer, 1980).

As the author sees it, it is possible to distinguish between 8 different characteristics of a scapegoat. He mentions the following types:

1. **The socially ineffective pupil**: These try to be accepted by their fellow pupils, but do this in strange, naive and inadequate ways. They have not learned how to behave in social situations.

2. **Family scapegoat and school scapegoat**: Typical of this is the child who has not learned social skills at home, and how to 'survive' outside the home.

3. **The 'Other' pupil**: Those who are different either because of their looks, hairstyle, clothes, behaviour, speech, habits, values, etc.

4. **The dirty pupil**: Pupils who are said not to wash, who look dirty or who smell.

5. **The tattle-talers**: Pupils who tell stories about other pupils to the teachers.

6. **The attention-seekers**: Pupils who like to be the center of attraction.

7. **Those who 'buy-off'**: These pupils buy candy and presents for their classmates in order to keep away from the bullying scene.

8. **The follower**: They obey all orders from their classmates. If they do not obey, they will be scapegoated.

Of course there are many pupils who are more a mixture of the above or who don't fit in at all. These categories simply provide a working model. Similar categories were reported by Hertroys and Kersten (1985). They used such names as 'Popeye', 'He-man', 'the follower', 'the fearful person', 'the badly tempered person' and 'the robot' to describe which characteristics they saw as prevalent in children who were bullied.

Management of bullying

Siffels and van Beek (1984), Hertroys and Kersten (1985) and van der Meer (1988) have all given some pointers on how to deal with the phenomenon of bullying. They all agree that this is a kind of behaviour that should not be tolerated, but are somewhat different in their approach.

Siffels and van Beek (1984) advocate the more harsh kind strategy; 'hit them hard', 'give them hell' are the kinds of advice we find in their article. This may seem quite drastic to some, but nevertheless, it might be better than just closing your eyes and letting everything continue. Bullying will not stop as long as nothing is done about it. Instead, the bullies will just see how far they can go before the scapegoat reacts. They will make things worse and are satisfied only when tears fall.

Another quote from this article: 'The reason why some children are never bullied is probably the strength and self-confidence that they have.' Support for this theory has been found in the works of Scandinavian researchers (see for instance Roland 1983). There it has been found that excessive fear or anger may entice the bully to keep on bullying. Reacting with fear or anger may indicate that the child is not self-confident. On the other hand, if a child is able to react 'correctly', this may indicate that the child is confident in his or her own actions.

Also, Roland (1987) has found that popularity is a key factor in who is bullied and who isn't. By popularity we here understand that a child has close friends. Roland found a great difference in measuring popularity. If you simply count how many choices a child receives, the result may be that also bullies are quite popular, however less popular than those not involved in bullying (Olweus 1974; Ekman 1977; Lagerspetz et al. 1982). If one counts the number of mutual choices (Peter chooses Paul and Paul chooses Peter), the picture can become quite different. In Rolands's study he found that both bullies and victims have fewer close friends than those not involved in bullying and that bullies were no more popular in that sense than victims.

Still, Siffels and van Beek do not draw these conclusions. Nor do they stress the importance of ego-picture and how to achieve a positive ego-picture for the pupils in the class. Instead, they say 'Sometimes it is a good idea to give children judo lessons or to give them a big dog.' A timid boy may well have a big dog. This is not an adequate way of helping the child face life at school or outside the home.

Jan Bart Hertroys and Wim Kersten (1985) do not reject aggressive behaviour as an answer to aggression either. 'Sometimes you will have to fight to keep your place in a group or to change your place in the group.' However, they do not propose that violence is the only solution, nor that it will always work. In some cases, for instance when being called names, they say that the child must consider the consequences of his behaviour. If you pick a fight or throw things, you might be 'sorry later'. In some cases, to show no reaction is the most effective way to put a stop to bullying, they say.

Hertroys and Kersten propose the use of role-play as a way to learn how to behave in various situations. This is a way to make things clearer for the young children and to let them find out what bullying really is. Bob van der Meer agreees in this. He too proposes role-play as a means to combat bullying. Through this type of activity, the children are given the chance to try different roles and to practice favourable behaviour.

In van der Meer's view (1988), the most important thing to do, is to take the problems seriously. The children he interviewed for his book, told him very clearly that the school often makes mistakes in their way of dealing with this problem. We need a clearer view on how to deal with this, clear strategies on how to help pupils, how to converse about the subject in the classroom. We need good lessons on war and peace as a starting point for the children to talk about their 'war'. Here role-plays can be central.

Van der Meer is convinced that the bullying problem has a lot to do with the relations between teacher, child and parent(s). The solution always has to do with this relationship. We need to work more on this so we can obtain a good and open relationship in this triad.

Also, it is important that the classroom atmosphere is warm and friendly. A classroom should look and feel like a home. Teachers should not only teach, but should be friends to the children. The pupils must be able to feel that they trust their teachers so that they dare admit to having problems – also outside school – and can discuss this with their teacher.

However, a problem that we face in Holland is that it is not uncommon for a primary school class to have three or four teachers. Which teacher should the pupils then contact? Which one do they know well enough – if any.

It is obvious then that there are many things we can grab hold of and work on to create better conditions for our pupils. It would be very positive if it were possible to create smaller classes and have fewer teachers involved with the lower grades. Scandinavian research has not found any connection between the size of the class and the amount of bullying (Olweus 1974). Still, the amount of material and research that has been carried out is little. Also, it is evident that although the number of pupils does not affect the amount of bullying, it must be much easier to do something about the problem and to work with it in smaller classes where the teacher is more able to pay attention to the individual. This is however an economic question.

Conclusion

We cannot give up the struggle for a better school, a safer school for our children, one in which they do not have to fear being scapegoated. In Holland, there has been much interest in this topic the last year. Since the problem reached the media, Bob van der Meer and myself have received a

58

never-ending stream of letters and phone calls about bullying. Articles are being published, lectures are being held. Perhaps in the not too distant future, we will know more about the problem in Holland and have clearer steps on how to deal with bullying in our society.

References

Bieneman, G. (1987) *De zondebok van de klas*. Elsevier.
de Kruif, N. (1987) *Is de treitertrend eeen Europees verschijnsel?* PCO-magazine.
de Kruif, N. (1988) *De treitertrend*. AO-reeks no. 2207, Stichting IVIO, Lelystad.
Ekman, K. (1977) *Skolemobbing*, Åbø, Åbø Akademi.
Hertroys, G.B. & Kersten, W. (1985) *Binken en Bangeriken, methodische beinvloeding van aggressief gedrag bij jeugdigen*. Haarlem.
Lagerspetz, K.M.. Bjørkqvist, K., Berts, M. & King, E. (1982) *Group aggression among school children in three schools*, Scandinavian Journal of Psychology 23, pp. 45–52.
Olweus, D. (1980) *Familial and temperamental determinants of aggressive behavior in adolescent boys: A causal analysis*. Developmental Psychology. no. 16, 644–660.
Roland, E. (1983) *Strategi mot mobbing*. Universitetsforlaget, Oslo.
Roland, E. (1987) Lectures held at the Council of Europe's Conference 'Bullying in School'. Stavanger, Norway.
van der Meer, B. (1988) *De zondebok in de klas*. Lens-reeks van het K.P.C. te Den Bosch.
van der Velden, R. (1987) *Pesten verpest het leren*. De Stem.

CHAPTER 5

Bullying in Italy

Sergio Basalisco

I When grown-ups are bullies

Faster and faster, the world is becoming something like McLuhan's village, and it is therefore quite likely that there aren't many differences between the countries of industrial and post-industrial areas. However, the increasing interest in childhood problems may be seen today as a peculiar feature of Italy. Children's conditions have slowly achieved a central position in the awareness of the Italian society, owing to the technical contribution of psychic development studies (pedagogics, psychology and psycho-analysis) and the increasing welfare which allows adults to devote more attention to children and childhood. In particular, people are now more sensitive towards mal-treated children.

Some researchers estimate that 15.000 children suffer from violence (physical, sexual or psychological) in Italy every year. But to these cases must be added other – and not less dangerous – forms of psychological and pedagogical abuse; children who are forsaken or left alone a number of hours in front of a television set, children who are shown no interest in their deepest needs, children who live under stressing rhythms of life owing to reasons of family prestige and success, a large number of children that drop out of compulsory school (about 100.00 every year), unlawful and unprotected child labour. Nearly 60.000 minors are still a victim of institutional violence. They are forsaken in institutions despite a recent law which encourages the entrustment of children to adoptive families where children might live in a climate of greater psychological welfare.

During these last years, research carried out by psychologists and paediatrists pointed out the prevalence of parents cruelties towards children. Violent parents' are not just psychopaths or a person altered by drugs or alcohol; violent people are distributed in every environment and social class. Violence often rises from intolerance towards a son/daughter seen as being 'trouble-some', 'naughty', 'dirty', 'crying and shrieking continuously' (Carloni-Nobili, 1982). Of this violence bursting inside the family, Ernesto Caffo, professor of childhood psychopathy at the University of Modena, wrote: 'Childhood is the weakest ring in society, group and family. Therefore every tension often discharges on it . . . .The child must fulfil the obligations proposed and imposed by his parent, who looks at the son as a dreadful competitor for the affective and social role that the parent will, or must, achieve. In this parent's opinion the child must reach at any rate social development and integration. If the child fails in his duty and shows "normal" behaviour as a child, his parent feels the son as somebody acting against him provocatively . . . .All these negative messages will follow the child during his development and will induce him when he becomes a parent, to pour them on his own child. . .'(Caffo, 1987)

There is an obvious difficulty in elaborating and practising a new culture enabling children to gain equality and subjectivity. Those opposed to the 'class society', for instance, have never succeeded in recognizing – as they ought – that if there are five classes in decreasing order of income, children are the sixth one, without income. It may be that Italy has a culture of family, but it is lacking a real culture of respect for the child as a person, based on solidarity and non-possession.

Is violence towards young people increasing? It is difficult to maintain this with any certainty. There is more awareness and more attention. The 'under 18 news collection' published by C.G.D. (an association of democratic parents), records all the articles about children from 0 to 18 years of age which have appeared in the six greatest Italian newspapers. In an item referring to 'violence on childhood' we find 19 news items in May 1987 in comparison with 2 news reports only in May 1982. The mass media do not keep silent any longer. The mass media are, without any doubt, very important in informing public opinion about events of macro and micro violence against Italian children. But there is a risk of unintelligent use of mass-media: a generic and superficial denunciation which raises a momentary pity, or the trend to create scandals without analyzing and without mobilizing the public opinion's criticism. Information about childhood must become an instrument to analyze a very complex reality which requires a careful and close investigation.

However, this greater public attention has contributed to multiplying the number of interventions in recent years. The Italian government appointed the National Board on Children Problems (1985) which is charged to supply the government with proposals and suggestions about childhood politics. The Board is now studying how to spread a new culture ('Grown-ups at the disposal of young people') to overcome the old culture which still prompts school selection and social isolation of youngsters. The Board has chosen two fields of intervention:

1. The right to socialization and education

Teenagers are particularly exposed to strong and misleading contradictions (welfare and crisis of ethical values, material overprotection and lack of autonomy, political freedom and subtle control of information) that may produce an unsafe future, poor relationships and loneliness. The aim of the new interventions is to increase the opportunities of playing, meeting, spending holidays together and international exchange; to support children's and youngsters' associations and out-of-school activities; to prevent school demotivation and failure.

2. The right to protection

The aim is to replace youth prison (based on law of the dictatorial period) with social control by which young people can really rid themselves of maladaptation; to protect children and teenagers who risk exploitation, sexual abuse, rejection because they belong to discriminated groups such as immigrants, gypsies, and so on.

This new philosophy of social rehabilitation has inspired a number of actions. Three years ago, a judge in Parma found an interesting alternative to youth prison: two boys, aged 16, who had unintentionally killed another youngster during a row among spectators at a football match, were sentenced to devote their free time to the assistance of old people and to give the victim's part of their wages for a certain number of years.

UNICEF Italian Committee is actively working to reaffirm Child's Rights and in more than 12.000 schools, it is carrying out a campaign to sensitize pupils and families. This included spreading many tens of thousands of copies of a special dossier 'Violence on children: Italian case' in November 1987.

In May 1987, a European meeting on 'Families in difficulties and child protection' was organized by the Italian Association Against Abuse on Childhood in the Lombardia region. The arguments of the conference were that it is wrong to look for the violent roots among children in the dissolution of the traditional family. It was argued that a child can grow up fine also in families with parents who are single, mentally ill, drug abusers, sniffers, prisoners, immigrants. As mentioned above, the real reasons are in a culture which is found in all social situations. Blaming so called 'problem groups' is not the answer. In a lot of towns, boards and associations have created 'blue telephones' to let people report cases of violence on children. In Bologna, this phone rang nearly 6000 times in 3 months during the summer of 1987, and 10% of the cases were serious enough to be entrusted to the social service's care.

II When children are bullies

At present, children's violence against other children is not perceived by the public.

However, increasing incidents reported by newspapers show that bullying among youngsters is an unexplored reality. For example:

1. On April 24, 1987, at Caserta (a small town near Naples), Roberto (age 15) wrote a letter to his parents: 'At school I do not succeed, I am daily taunted by one teacher and my mates. I feel a deep sense of failure.' Then he killed himself with his father's gun. School failure and psychic violence raised a strong wish for death in Roberto who was very fond of electronics and photography in his spare time and who had all the features for being normally happy.

2. In Rome, a mother very ill and deserted by her husband, sheltered one of her many children in an institute. Michele, 11 years old, was given a hamster by his parish priest. The child, fearing his mates would kill the little pet, asked his mother to take the hamster home, in vain. So Michele ran away from the institute in which he had been living for three years but where he could no longer live feeling he was violently harassed (May 20, 1987).

3. On the same day in Naples, a girl aged 13 revealed to her teacher that she had been injected with heroin by a mate of hers for a long time, and that lately he expected her to prostitute herself.

Knowledge that there is concern among children was obtained in a very interesting investigation by the UNICEF Committee in Sassari in 1987. Primary school pupils (aged 6–11) were invited to write a composition: 'Difficulties and expectations of my life as a child in family, school, and society.'

Some of the results were:

From 500 compositions it turned out that 80% of the children live 'normally', while 20% perceive trouble.

Of these 20% who perceived trouble:

70% was attributed to;
- lack of communication at home
- disagreement between parents
- physical violence
- loneliness
- rivalry among brothers

10% was attributed to playing an inferior role at home.
20% was attributed to bullying and difficulties at school.

These 20% represent 4% of the total number of pupils who wrote an essay on this topic. This must be said to be an alarming number of children seeing as they were free to write about anything under the theme of difficulties and expectations which is a rather broad theme. We can only speculate on what the percentage would be had the composition been given about bullying specifically. Perhaps we can say that the amount of bullying might be somewhere along the results that have been reached in other countries – about 10%.

Monica, aged 10, wrote: 'My mates don't love me, I feel forsaken, they mock me because they say I am fat. Nobody wants me to play and I don't know what to do.'

In terms of the range of children's fears, bullying is not the most frequently cited. In a study by the C.G.D. (Parents' Association) of 18.000 children aged 6–11 years carried out in 1987, war, adult violence, drug pushers and reproaches from teachers all featured strongly. But for the victim of bullying it is an immediate threat as Monica testifies.

III What can we do about bullying?

The cases of bullying I observed during my professional experience (as a headteacher in a junior high school, with 11–14 year old pupils) were decidedly few in country schools, but in recent years, working in suburban schools, I had the opportunity to notice that these situations were less uncommon. I think it is useful to refer to an example:

Lorenzo, a 13 year old boy in a class of pupils aged 11, was fourth among six brothers and had a father who, owing to his job (night watchman), could not have a good relationship with his children or the school. The boy was of limited intelligence and attention span, and was not very fond of studies. His school results were poor. Lorenzo used to express domineering attitudes towards his school-friends, particularly towards a boy and a girl with a slight mental handicap. Every demand for collaboration addressed to his family was useless as his father's solution to all problems was to beat the boy very severely. Some results were achieved by those teachers who developed relationships with Lorenzo based on firmness and trust.

Generally bullying and harassing attitudes among pupils become less evident when the school increases the opportunity for pupils to partake in school life and organisation, for instance by encouraging classes in turn to keep order during breaks, sightseeing tours and sports meetings. Class meetings when pupils, parents and teachers gather to discuss and think over problematic behaviour, have also proved useful.

In Italy, primary school (since 1985) and secondary school (since 1979) syllabuses have been giving more prominence to education on how to live in the community. This is based on acceptance and respect for others in order to counteract prejudice towards other people and cultures. Additionally, experience from 'peace education' has stressed the containment of aggressive instincts in human relationships. The curriculum on social education developed by the teachers of a primary and a secondary school at Gemona (Friuli, north-eastern Italy) provides an example of this approach.

Children in the primary school are to be helped

To recognize their own needs, but also the need for self control.
To accept other children's opinions.
To express feelings, emotions and experiences.
To lend things to others and to respect school material.
To listen to others and take turns to speak.
To accept also the proposals that are different from theirs.
To cooperate in planning and to take engagements, accepting help from others when necessary.
To play with other children and be willing to change roles.
To invite girls and boys who are excluded.
To specify the reasons for behaviour.

Children in the secondary school are to be helped

To express personal opinions about events, also when their

opinions are different than others.
To consider what is proposed.
To give cooperation.
To assess behaviour.
To accept all others and devote attention to what they say and propose.
To be tolerant towards those who are physically, socially and culturally different.
To learn to change individual proposals in order to achieve a collective effort.

Conclusion

It is through a curriculum based on the idea that children do not have to be aggressive, that they can learn strategies of negotiation, give up self-centred perspectives, and understand other people's beliefs, that bullying will be tackled.

References

Caffo, E. (1987) *Quarto, onora il padre: il genitore, un modello impossible e violento*, in 'Il manifesto', 12 May.
Carloni-Nobili, (1982) *La mamma cattiva*, Guaraldi (ed.) Firenze.

CHAPTER 6

Bullying in Scandinavia

Elaine Munthe

Introduction

The Scandinavian countries and Finland all have a long tradition of welfare and of common concern among the inhabitants. Looking back in time, it is obvious that a small country like Norway with only 4.1 million inhabitants today, had to care for its people in order to grow and thrive. Nowadays, much time and money is spent on considering processes and measures to ensure safety, happiness, health, etc.

In the following I will present the Norwegian school system as an example of the Scandinavian school system. There are of course differences between the systems preferred in each country, but these differences are not that major.

As we will see, our school system also reflects this ideology of common concern. We want our pupils to feel safe at school, to feel close to those working with them and their classmates. Therefore, we strive to keep classes in Norway permanent from 1st grade through 9th. In more rural areas where the children go to smaller schools during the first years and are later 'rounded up' at larger junior high schools, one must mix the classes in order to form larger ones. So in these and similar cases, pupils will get new classmates at a later stage.

We also strive to keep the same teacher from 1–6 grade. When the pupils change school in the 7th grade, they will usually have one teacher who is 'theirs' – their homeroom teacher – but also a group of other teachers. Still, most schools try to keep the number of teachers per class as low as possible.

The school system can be described as follows:

67

Figure 6.1: The Norwegian School System.

Age	Grade	
18	12	
17	11	OPTIONAL
16	10	
15	9	
14	8	COMPULSORY
13	7	
12	6	
11	5	
10	4	COMPULSORY
9	3	
8	2	
7	1	
6	Preschool	OPTIONAL

A good class and school ethos is particularly stressed as being very important to achieve, and much work is devoted to this. The Norwegian curriculum plan for the elementary and secondary schools, stresses the importance of children learning tolerance, learning to take responsibility for themselves and others and caring for each other (Mønsterplan 1987). This is evident in the School Law of 13 June 1969 which also emphasizes that the school should enhance intellectual freedom and tolerance.

This plus the fact that we live in a relatively quiet part of the world – with no revolutions, no harsh leaders, no poverty of any great measure – could be some of the reasons why it was in Sweden that the interest in bullying started and that it spread quickly to the neighbouring countries.

One of the reasons why the concept of bullying caught on among the public could be that it is indeed a recognizable problem. Most people have experienced it as an on-looker or as a partaker (either bully or victim). It is a problem parents understand, one they can remember or even live through to this day. Therefore, parents grasped this problem and eagerly participated in discussions around it.

The history behind bullying as a field of research and concern started in 1969 – about 20 years ago – with Peter Paul Heinemann, a Swedish doctor who was walking past a school when he saw some pupils in the playground. He decided to take a closer look at what they were up to and discovered that one of the boys in the group was being chased by the others. The boy ran right out of his sandal, leaving it behind in the sandbox where Dr. Heinemann could later pick it up, hold it, and remember his own childhood years. (Heinemann, 1973).

He called it 'mobbing', a term he borrowed from the studies of animals (Lorenz 1968). Heinemann understands 'mobbing' as group violence directed against a deviant individual. He sees it as group behaviour that occurs suddenly and subsides suddenly, bringing everything back to normal again.

Definition of bullying

This brings us right to the core of the problem of definition. What is this phenomenon of bullying? Is it necessarily only group violence? Can't there be instances where a single child (or adult) bullies another?

The question is really whether one wishes to emphasize the number of agents carrying out the act, or the act itself. The Scandinavian term 'mobbing' does imply that there are several members in a group. This meaning is missing in the English word 'bullying'. However, for the victim it can be of less importance *how many*. It is the *what* and the *result* that matters the most. Yet there are several opinions in this matter (see for example the chapter by Pikas). Therefore, a good definition is necessary to clarify what the researcher really understands by bullying.

If we take a look at the 'what', we find there are several ways to bully others. Heinemann first observed a gang of boys chasing a single boy. Physical violence is one means. Psychological violence is another; taunting school-mates, mocking them, teasing them. Another example of psychological violence is the use of exclusion. By this we understand the act in which a pupil is first led to believe that there is a possibility of his/her joining a particular group, but then being excluded from its activities after all.

One distinction that is very important to make in this definition, is the aspect of time. Bullying does not mean that one or more persons tease another friend once in a blue moon. Bullying is something that occurs *regularly*. As with most terms that become popular, bullying – mobb(n)ing in Scandinavian – has lost a lot of its meaning. It is used about everything and often in a joking way. Therefore, many pupils also think of mobbing as something minor, something everybody does. This the researcher or observer/teacher must be aware of. It makes it very important for especially the researcher, to stress what is understood, and that in research mobbing is understood as actions that take place regularly and over time.

Another distinction we must make is that of *balance*. It is not called bullying if two equally strong (physically or mentally) pupils have a fight or quarrel. In a bullying situation there is always one part who is stronger than the other. This becomes evident in the reactions of the victim – he or she is not able to defend themselves in the actual situation.

We have now reached the point where we are able to formulate a definition of bullying: 'Bullying is longstanding violence, either physical or psychological, conducted by an individual or a group and directed against an individual who is not able to defend himself in the actual situation' (Roland 1987).

Thus we have reached a formal definition of this phenomenon, but what is it that actually takes place in a bullying situation?

Most bullies are aware of the fact that bullying is not an acceptable behaviour (Roland 1980). They know what the norms are and if spoken to about this behaviour, they will often agree completely that bullying 'isn't nice.' Yet they do bully others.

One method they can use to justify their own behaviour, is to '*legalize*' their actions (Roland 1983). A good picture of this is given in the 1983 videofilm made by A/S Vida and subsidized by the Norwegian Ministry of Education; 'Mobbing – Scenes from the everyday life of children.' In one of these cuts we see a young boy bicycling off from school with his trumpet on the back of his bike. Two other boys are waiting for him, and as he leaves they start their pursuit of him. The chase is a dramatic one; Dag, the boy being pursued looks behind his back continuously. He is overtaken, pushed off his bike and his trumpet is taken away.

'Give me back my trumpet!' he says to the bullies.

One of the boys grabs him by his arm and twists his arm while the other says:

'That's not a polite way to ask! Say: Could you please give me back my trumpet?'

Here, the boys are given an 'excuse' for their bullying behaviour. Of course they should help improve Dag's manners, it's their duty.

In other cases, it might be the bully who bumps into the victim but who puts the blame on the victim. 'Can't you walk decently?' 'Stop bumping into me every time I see you!' The actual situation is *distorted*, and this is a very useful method for children to use so that they can legalize their behaviour for themselves and others (Roland 1983).

Two interesting decades

The years after Heinemann published his first article in 1969 have not been futile ones. Much energy has been spent on trying to develop ways of combatting this violence which is found among children and adults.

The public was made aware of the problem and that in itself is positive.

Newspapers, radio and television showed an enormous interest in this field. This interest which led to many articles, news reports etc. was of great value in spreading information about the problem of bullying. Only when we are aware of something, have given it a name, can we do something about it.

Researchers in Sweden, Finland, Denmark and Norway have dealt with this problem in different ways. Various methods of collecting information have been used: questionnaires, interviews, observations. Some have concentrated on the empirical side of this work, others have tried to come with more practical ideas for teachers, and in Norway the government also decided to intervene and try to do something by initiating a national campaign against bullying in 1983.

All of this would probably not have happened had the results of research been otherwise. However, researchers did find that bullying is and was a serious problem for schoolchildren. If we look at the research that has been carried out and try to estimate an average percentage, we will find that at least 5% of the Scandinavian elementary and secondary school children are regularly bullied at school or on their way to and from school, and about the same number of pupils are involved as bullies (See figures 6.2 and 6.3 below). In numbers, Professor Dan Olweus, University of Bergen, calculated that 80 thousand Norwegian schoolchildren were involved in bullying in 1983 (Olweus, 1985).

From the following tables we can read the percentage of girls and boys who reported being victimized or being bullies in several of the Scandinavian investigations undertaken since 1969.

Figure 6.2: Results on percentage of pupils involved in bullying: the victims

Researchers and Year	Girls	Boys	Frequency
Pedersen 1975	5.9	9.2	Sometimes
Ekman 1977	2.7	5.7	Sometimes – often
Mykletun 1979	8.0	12.3	Often
Roland 1980	14.8	26.7	Every week
Meltveit Kleppa & Endresen 1980	6.9	11.5	Every week
Vignes Steine & Aukland 1980	8.0	13.7	Every week
Bjørkqvist et al. 1982	2.7	5.7	Sometimes – often
Lagerspetz et al. 1982	2.2	5.7	Sometimes – often
Olweus 1985	8.0	10.0	Sometimes – more often

(Roland 1987)

Figure 6.3: Results on percentage of pupils involved in bullying: the bullies

Researchers and Year	Girls	Boys	Frequency
Pedersen 1975	0.6	3.1	–
Ekman 1977	3.2	9.6	Sometimes
Mykletun 1979	5.7	17.9	–
Roland 1980	1.6	9.4	Every week
Meltveit Kleppa & Endresen 1980	4.6	7.6	Every week
Vignes Steine & Aukland 1980	0.4	0.8	Often – very often
Bjørkqvist et al. 1982	3.2	9.6	Sometimes – often
Lagerspetz et al. 1982	3.2	8.0	Sometimes – often
Olweus 1985	3.5	11.0	Sometimes – more often

(Roland 1987)

Who are the bullies and the victims?

Unfortunately, we cannot give a clear picture of who the bullies are. This is because the group is a diverse one. Some of the bullies are regarded as very resourceful children, popular, managing well scholastically (Olweus, 1978). Others are less successful, less popular than others. According to Olweus, their position in the bullying group may have something to do with it. Those bullies who play central roles are the most resourceful whereas those who are more peripheral are also more complex. If we take a look at group dynamics in connection with this, it becomes obvious that the more popular ones are the central figures, and if this is to be a bullying group, then the most popular ones must be the strongest bullying agents.

As concerns the victims, researchers have found more stable findings. Although in some cases you might have what has long been considered the "typical" victim; a short/weak/bespectacled/freckled/fat child, there are other children with similar looks who are *not* victimized (Olweus 1978). One has, however, found that a large amount of victims are rather uncertain children with a low ego picture (Mykletun 1979) who feel that their being bullied is deserved more than other children. (Roland 1983). The victims' academic achievement has also been found lower than that of children not involved in bullying (Olweus 1978, Mykletun 1979, Roland 1980).

Olweus (1978) mentions two kinds of victims: the quiet ones and the provocative ones. The quiet victims are innocent, meaning that his being bullied has nothing to do with his behaviour prior to the bullying situation. This is the largest group. The provocative victim, which is not that usual, shows some unfortunate behaviour that provokes children into bullying this child.

Another matter which further confuses our categorical way of thinking is that many bullies are also victims (Roland 1980). It has been calculated that about one fourth of the bullies are also to be found among the victims. (See also O'Moore's chapter in this volume).

Home environment

Olweus has mostly studied boy-bullies and has found that their home environment is often a violent one. The boys' fathers often use violent means of punishing their child, and the result of this could be reflected in the fact that the boy again uses violence towards others (1980). This is a similar reaction as that which we find among children who are molested at home and who, as adults, also molest their children.

A second item of importance which Olweus has reported in his 1980 publication is how the relationship between parent and child can influence the child's use of aggression. In his study, he found that the more negative a mother (in all of these cases it was the mother who was most responsible for the child's upbringing) is towards her child, the more aggressive the child would be. Also, those mothers who were most lenient as to controlling aggressive behaviour from their children, had the most aggressive children. (Olweus 1980).

Girl bullies we know little about as concerns home environment, so here there is still work to be done before we can say anything certain about their situation.

As for socio-economic status, results have been quite contradictory and thus it remains difficult to say anything for certain about this in Scandinavia. Mykletun (1979) and Olweus (1978) found no connections between the parents' socio-economic status and their child's participation in bullying. Roland (1980) did however find that children of parents with either little or much schooling (little = less than 9 years, much = 14 or more years) were bullied the most, and that children of fathers who had little schooling were more likely to be bullies. It is, on the basis of these investigations, too early to say whether the factor of socio-economic status plays any part in bullying in Scandinavia.

Another family matter that has been investigated by several researchers it to what degree children who are bullies or victims are together with their parents and what these relationships are like.

Vignes Steine & Aukland (1980) report that victims tend to spend more time with their parents than other children do. What this means can of

study bullying among ca. 7.000 pupils (aged 8–16) at 37 different schools in Rogaland, Norway. Three years prior to the Janus Project, the same schools had participated in using the exact same questionnaire among their pupils. Then it was Professor Dan Olweus of the University of Bergen who was responsible for the investigation which had been requested by the Ministry of Education and he was thus responsible for designing the questionnaire which we also used.

The Ministry of Education was interested in a follow-up of the 1983 survey. Erling Roland applied for and received the project. The project period has lasted a total of three and a half years including the 1/2-year start-up period. In December 1988 it came to an end and the results expressly asked for by the Ministry of Education were reported on, whereas several others are still being analyzed.

As stated earlier, bullying is a topic which has been focussed on a great deal in the Scandinavian countries. In Norway the Ministry of Education even initiated a nationwide campaign against bullying in which all schools were invited to participate (1983).

However, our results from the Janus project which compare findings from 1983 with the results from 1986 indicate that there is no less bullying among school children now than in 1983. Quite the contrary.

From figure 6.5 we can see that the amount of bullying has in fact increased over the three-year period. But is it so certain that this has happened despite all the efforts made?

When looking closer at the data collected, we have found that there is great variance from school to school. One tendency is that those schools that had little bullying in 1983 also have little bullying in 1986. Additionally, there is some evidence that schools which took an active part in the campaign produced better results (Roland, 1988). So some schools are for some reason or other better off than others in this respect. Obviously, there are some schools factors involved that can influence the amount of bullying taking place. We have included data on staff co-operation, teaching methods preferred, classroom management, etc. and hope to look at bullying under this light as well.

Our findings have however shown that the amount of bullying taking place in schools around in Rogaland has not increased for both sexes.

As we can read from figure 6.6, girls report bullying others about the same in 1986 as in 1983, they report on being bullied less in 1986 and also on being excluded less. If we take a look at the percentage of boys who have answered that they have been bullied, have been excluded and have bullied others *once a week or more often*, we will see that there has been an increase for all three categories.

If we choose to follow Roland's hypothesis (1987) mentioned above,

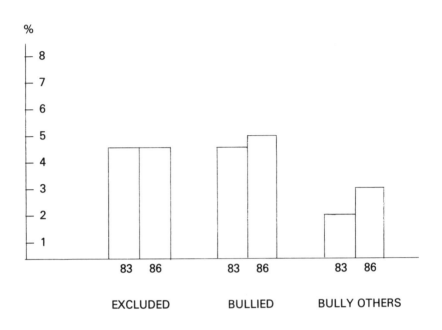

Figure 6.5: Bullying in 1983 and 1986. 4th-9th graders from 37 schools in Rogaland, Norway. Total percentage. Once a week or more often.

Figure 6.6: Boys and girls, grades 4-9. Results from the Janus Project. Once a week or more often.

	Girls		Boys	
	83	86	83	86
Excluded	5.4%	5.0%	4.0%	4.5%
Bullied	4.0%	3.5%	3.6%	5.2%
Bully others	0.7%	0.8%	4.1%	5.1%

we can try to explain these findings by referring to the sex differences in how one bullies. As we can see, exclusion has remained more or less stable from 1983 to 1986 whereas the more physical kind of bullying has increased. Girls tend to bully among their own female classmates, whereas boys bully boys and girls from within or outside their own school-class. Boys bully others more than girls do and in a more physical way than girls. 5.2% of the boys say they have been bullied once a week or more often in 1986 and they have been bullied mostly by other boys.

The girls, who report less bullying in 1986 than in 1983 have been bullied by girls and boys then, but there is a decline over this period.

Conclusion

Research into bullying over the last 20 years has mainly been focussed on the individuals involved; the bully and his/her victim. Researchers have strived to find out more about *why* some children become bullies and others become victims by taking a closer look at their personalities, their physical appearances, their scholastic achievements, their popularity among others, etc. Some investigations have dealt with familial matters.

Recently, 'The Janus Project' is an example of the trend of Scandinavian research to start looking elsewhere. We have tried to look at bullying within a more global approach, taking into consideration the personal factors that have been found, but placing these in a larger context. We have moved a step or two outside the bullying unit itself to take a look at other social instances that may influence this bullying unit. The school as a whole, for instance: Can co-operation between the teachers or between the teachers and the administration have any influence on how much bullying goes on at a particular school? Can teachers' engagement in their profession have any impact on bullying? Will teaching methods used in a particular class enhance bullying?

We are all too aware of the fact that bullying is a problem in our schools and for our children. It has been necessary to investigate the mechanisms involved in bullying and the children themselves so as to learn more about how to deal with this problem so that we could stop it. Now we are facing another step and another challenge; taking a closer look at the systems around the children that may influence their behaviour and trying to find solutions that will prevent bullying from occurring in the first place.

References

Bjørkqvist, K., Ekman, K. & Lagerspetz, K. (1982) *Bullies and victims: Their ego picture, ideal ego picture and normative ego picture.* Scandinavian Journal of Psychology 23, 307–313.

Ekman, K. (1977) *Skolemobbing.* Åbø: Åbø Akademi.

Heinemann, P. P. (1973) *Mobbing. Gruppevold blant barn og voksne.* Oslo: Gyldendal.

Lagerspetz, K. M., Bjørkqvist, K., Berts, M. & King, E. (1982) *Group aggression among school children in three schools.* Scandinavian Journal of Psychology 23, 45–52.

78

Lorenz, K. (1968) *Den såkalte ondskap. Om aggresjon hos mennesker og dyr.* Oslo: Cappelen.

Meltveit Kleppa, M. & Endresen, S. (1980) *Ein analyse av forhold som gjeld trivsel og mobbing ved Hjelmeland ungdomsskule.* Stavanger: Stavanger College of Education.

Mykletun, R. J. (1979) *Plaging i skolen.* Stavanger: Roga landsforskning.

Olweus, D. (1978) *Aggression in the schools. Bullies and whipping boys.* Washington D.C.: Hemisphere Press.

Olweus, D. (1980) *Familial and temperamental determinants of aggressive behaviour in adolescent boys: A causal analysis.* Development Psychology 16, 644–660.

Olweus, D. (1985) *80.000 elever innblandet i mobbing.* Norsk Skoleblad No. 2.

Pedersen, J. R. (1975) *Mobning blandt skoleelever.* Aarhus: Aarhus Universitet.

Roland, E. (1980) *Terror i skolen.* Stavanger: Roga landsforskning.

Roland, E. (1983) *Strategi mot mobbing.* Oslo: Universitetsforlaget.

Roland, E. (1987) Lectures held at the Council of Europe's Conference on 'Bullying in School', Stavanger 1987.

Vignes Steine, M. & Aukland, R. (1980) *Offer og plager i ulike sammenhenger.* Stavanger: The Stavanger College of Education.

PART II

Approaches to Dealing with Bullying

CHAPTER 7

Management Strategies with Vulnerable Children

Valerie Besag

Introduction

An overview of research specific to bullying and to related areas indicates those factors which contribute to some children being at risk of becoming involved in a bullying situation in school. A mesh of familial, tempera-mental, environmental and sociological factors appears to predispose some children to become aggressors and others to be at risk of attack. (Besag, 1989). Any child could be caught up in a bullying attack by being in the wrong place at the wrong time in the wrong company, but those involved in prolonged or repeated bullying, aggressors or victims, would seem to possess identifiable characteristics which predispose them to being at risk. Some degree of long term socialization difficulties may have been noted by parents or teachers previous to the bullying incidents. Simply to halt the bullying, therefore, would be to leave the situation unresolved. Punishment meted out to the bullies may stop the bullying but would not tap the underlying problem of maladaptive social inter-actions.

Profiles drawn from the work of Olweus, 1978, would indicate bullies to be energetic, strong, well co-ordinated and confident. They are able to communicate effectively and are most often of average academic ability. Victims of bullying are less energetic, weaker, poorly co-ordinated and lacking in confidence. They communicate less effectively, often being withdrawn or isolated, and are able to offer only futile attempts to defend themselves verbally or physically.

The work initiated in school therefore needs to be addressed towards the code of conduct accepted as valid by the bullies, to their stage of moral development and to the sanctions and level of supervision which it may be necessary to impose on them for the protection of others. Work with the victims needs to be based on possible communication or co-ordination difficulties, the enhancement of friendship skills and the development of confidence and self esteem, in addition to specific advice on how to avoid or fend off confrontation and attack. Confidence would appear to be the one factor which most clearly differentiates bullies from their victims. The bullies, however, may not be confident within their own peer group, there they may be victims themselves, yet they may bully younger pupils or siblings.

Bullying, whether viewed from the position of aggressor or victim, is a multifactorial problem demanding a multidimensional response from the school. This response is perhaps most effective if considered in the areas of: prevention, investigation, protection, resolution and reparation.

Prevention

Preventative work is perhaps the most effective approach to take. Children at risk can be identified early in their school career and subsequently monitored. A variety of methodologies and research designs may be used to discover those children who fall into the high risk categories. Results from small scale research organized within individual schools such as: sociometric work, teacher or pupil questionnaires, analysis of friendship groups, playground and classroom observations, case studies and pupil tracking could be matched with the profiles of bullies and victims offered by the large scale research (Olweus, 1978) to identify potential problems.

Workshops for parents could alert them to warning signs and advice could be offered on how to cope if they suspect their child is bullying others or is being bullied. To discuss the problem openly should not cause undue anxiety as both pupils and parents are known to nominate bullying in schools as a priority concern. (Measor and Woods, 1984, Elliott, 1986).

Well established liaison links with feeder schools, infant or primary, and a comprehensive induction programme for all new pupils, would offer a degree of confidence to those apprehensive of change and go a long way towards identifying and halting problems in the embryonic stage.

Any sound preventive programme would need financial support. A well publicized and effective school policy, commitment to good architectural design, so that all areas of the school may be observed easily, and adequate levels of supervision to enable pupils to be protected effectively, not only on the school premises but in related situations such as on the school bus, all require adequate financial input. A poor staffing ratio, for example, could mean that children would be left without appropriate supervision in the case of staff absences or at the change over of lessons when staff may be unavoidably unpunctual to class due to distance between classrooms. Such circumstances offer opportunities for bullying to occur.

Vigilant supervision alone could be an effective preventative measure. Well supervised play areas, queues, changing rooms and corridors can contribute to a calm and purposeful atmosphere non-conducive to deviant behaviour. There is a growing interest in structured games and play activities being offered at free times in schools as unresolved conflicts are often carried over into fractious and disruptive outbursts in lesson time. Supervision need not be authoritarian or punitive but could be covert and constructive, for example, by staff chatting informally in corridors to pupils, offering leisure activities or helping older pupils to support younger ones.

A high level of professional practice maintained by all staff working as a mutually supportive team is a most effective way of keeping social and disciplinary problems to a minimum. Factors within individual schools, such as thorough preparation and attractive presentation of work, appropriate curriculum material, class routines and management practices and the quality of relationships between pupils and staff, have been found to be more influential to the eventual outcome of pupils than within child influences (Mortimore *et al.*, 1988). All these factors could be subsumed under the heading of good professional practice.

The relationship between pupils and staff could be of the utmost importance. Children are in school for a large part of most days and in contact with teachers who are able to draw upon their expertise to support them over a number of years. This prolonged contact may be the closest and most stable relationship some children experience. The role of the teacher in modelling appropriate responses and in facilitating and offering appropriate social interactions cannot be underestimated.

A highly competitive ethos in the school, so that only few are winners, could result in feelings of isolation, frustration and humiliation for those unable to succeed. A mismatch between curriculum and pupil could contribute to some considering themselves to be failures. The curriculum needs to be supportive and compensatory in the areas of social development and physical agility in addition to academic remediation. Socioeconomic pressures also need to be considered. Pupils leaving school without relevant skills and a realistic opportunity of obtaining the goals proffered by society, feeling inadequate to take their place in the world, could turn to aggression and conflict to ease their resentment or to change their situation.

The attitude of society to bullying needs to be urgently examined. As long as there is a heritage of opinion which considers that it can be sorted out among the children themselves, that it is a valuable learning experience, that we cannot and need not, as adults, do anything constructive to help, then bullying in schools is being covertly supported. Within the school a sense of community can be developed where all, pupils and staff, take responsibility for each other. If pupils witnessing bullying feel confident to alert staff in the context of taking responsible action, rather than telling tales, this could be a most powerful preventative strategy. If pupils are alerted to the subtleties of bullying so that they recognise it and can see that it is the dominance of the powerful over the powerless, and as such warrants no kudos, a change in attitude could be brought about. This community ethos has been successfully developed in some schools. A school for children with severe emotional and behavioural problems, Feversham School (M.I.N.D.) is such an establishment. All pupils and staff meet together twice a week to discuss and resolve difficulties in an open democratic forum. Not only staff feel responsible for the pupils for in this way all pupils are made aware of their responsibilities to each other.

Investigation

Any suspicion of bullying needs to be investigated with urgency and sensitivity. Parents or teachers who are aware that something is wrong but who are unable to elicit information from the child of concern, need to strongly suspect the possibility that the child is being bullied. In most cases the victim is unable to offer information due to fear, humiliation, embarrassment or confusion. It is more productive to seek information by observation, or from peers or their parents, than to persist in questioning the suspected victim. Children merely witnessing bullying are often afraid and disclose their anxieties to their parents. (Elliott 1986).

Care needs to be taken in defining whether or not it is a case of bullying or whether the claim of being bullied is providing an excuse for nonattendance. Conversely, girls particularly may be bullied without defining it as bullying as the form of bullying between girls is often covert, such as malicious gossip or social ostracism (Roland, 1988). A log kept of incidents such as temper outbursts, weepiness, truancy or loss of possessions could offer valuable insights into a pattern of behaviour and help identify the perpetrators. Older pupils may offer information without the risk of the reprisals the peer group may encounter. Older pupils have been successfully used to shadow victims to observe the interactions which take place when the bullies feel confident that they are not being observed by staff. One such example is the case of a young boy who refused to attend school but would give no reason. He became hysterical when coercive tactics were tried by his parents. It was eventually deduced by his parents and the school staff that he was being bullied but they could find no evidence. Two older pupils were assigned to shadow the boy and in the first break time these older pupils saw that he was being kept out of the cloakroom by two boys in his class. He had only two choices; to go out into the playground in the winter weather without a coat, or run the gauntlet of verbal and physical abuse if he went near the cloakroom. The boys were lying in wait each break time to trap him in the cloakroom where they had him at their mercy. Once the problem was identified by the older pupils and reported back, the culprits were chastised and the problem was resolved immediately. The exposure of the deviant behaviour was enough to prevent a further incident, but the older pupils did keep a watchful eye on the victim for some time, and an intermittent check was kept over a period of months until the young boy made friends with a group who were able to protect him if any further trouble occurred. Such strategies must be adopted in a most sensitive manner. These more confident or older pupils could remain to protect the victim, even when the bullies have been confronted, and could offer support in developing social and friendship skills until the victim is fully integrated in the class group. Further examples of peer support being used in such ways are given in Besag, 1989.

Resolution

The mode chosen for the resolution of the conflict could influence whether or not the aggressor and victim continue to have underlying social difficulties or whether the conflict resolution is a learning experience from which both benefit. The aggression of the bully could be modelled on behaviour within the home, it could be the 'modus operandi' of the street culture, or it could stem from a lack of empathic involvement between parent and child, what Olweus 1987 terms 'silent violence'. Sanctions and supervision alone could merely increase resentment. Before the aggressors can be expected to appreciate the feelings of others and demonstrate feelings of reciprocity, some understanding of the level of their moral development may be necessary (Kohlberg, 1981, Dewey, 1916). A most effective way of raising the stage of moral development of a child is by encouraging a community ethos in school. The victims will need help to develop skills to defend themselves and they may need guidance to reach a higher level of maturity and independence.

Conflict resolution can be an important learning experience, for example the contribution made by Walker to this volume. It is a here and now, pertinent problem to be resolved in a dynamic fashion. Many intellectual skills may be called upon in discussion or mediation. Specially trained peer mediators may be used to settle such disputes. (Shrief, 1988). A wide variety of responses which could be made need to be discussed in depth and evaluated and ordered, the opinions of others need to be sought and the range of possible outcomes of actions considered. The end product must be that both parties feel that there has been a successful resolution, that no-one has lost face, and no-one has been blamed or humiliated, and that a workable solution has been evolved so that both are able to face similar situations in the future, which will undoubtedly occur, with the skills to resolve them appropriately.

Reconciliation

The optimum outcome of any conflict situation would be to effect a reconciliation of the opposing factions so that not only is the specific conflict stopped but negative feelings which may have triggered the incidents are confronted and understood. Individual, peer or group counselling may be used to help aggressors and their victims to understand each other's point of view. The bully may better understand the problems a poorly co-ordinated child experiences, the victim may gain some insight into the behaviour of a bully who did not realise the distress taunting may cause. In my own experience such mutual understanding has been valuable and productive, but has only been achieved in cases where there has been no premeditated decision to severely hurt or humiliate the victim. If the bullies are using a different code of conduct and yardstick of success from that of the school and the victim, it will be necessary to turn, in the initial stages, to other techniques. Large group or class discussions, where the issue of bullying is discussed impartially without identified participants, have been found to be successful in some cases, possibly as the dimension of peer pressure is added. The bullies can see group opinion is against them and the intellectual arguments may be presented in an impersonal atmosphere. A better understanding of such phenomena as teasing, malicious gossip and social ostracism may be reached in a less threatening and confrontational atmosphere than in an individual or small group situation. A consensus of opinion could alter the attitude of the less intractible bullies or persuade a victim to conform more to the behaviour of the group. Advice imposed on pupils, however, is rarely adopted. Feelings of reciprocity and responsibility, integral to moral development, may be elicited from such discussions which are genuine manifestations of group feeling, whereas instruction or threat imposed by adults would be ignored. The case of a young girl in the first year at a secondary school offers a good example of this process. During a class discussion about bullying the young girl admitted that she was being bullied by a group of boys all of whom were present in the class. This disclosure came without preamble or prompting and the whole class was taken by surprise. The girl was obviously extremely upset by the bullying but the teacher had been unaware of the problem. The identified group of boys were defensive and explained that, although they had teased and taunted the girl, who had entered school from a different area, they had only called her names and, in their opinion, this could not be classed as bullying. The class discussion which ensued resulted in the boys coming to understand the distress their behaviour had caused and the difficulty was successfully resolved. Further examples of this type of work are given in Besag, 1989.

Reparation

Perhaps the most difficult goal to achieve is the long term remediation of the underlying difficulties which initially triggered the bullying. If these are not addressed research indicates that both bullies and their victims are at risk of continuing social problems in adulthood. (Olweus, 1988, Cowen, 1973, Lane, 1988). Understanding the behaviour of ourselves and others does not guarantee effective execution of appropriate action. Some support is often necessary to bring about change. Behavioural programmes can support the aggressors for each small step achieved towards mastering more appropriate social responses. A better relationship between teacher and child may result when the teacher is rewarding good behaviour, rather than punishing the bad. Praise is a powerful reinforcement for most children. The victims could be rewarded for mastering social hurdles as often after bullying incidents many situations prove too difficult for vulnerable children to cope with without strong support. Situations such as entering the dining hall, games lessons, walking among groups of children, speaking in front of the class, all demand courage to master once a child has lost confidence. The peer group could have an important part to play in effecting the successful reintegration of the vulnerable child into the group. Programmes designed to support children in re-entering groups are outlined in Besag, 1989. It may be that there are more opportunities for appropriate rewards to be given at home than in school, such as later bedtimes, extra time to watch T.V. pocket money etc. If this is so that behavioural programme can be run in conjunction with the parents who can use the rewards for success in school.

One important aspect of the social interactions of children is that of friendships and popularity. Children make a choice concerning who they will assist and who they will ignore. This is linked to the factors which discriminate between popular, non-popular and unpopular children. Those who are gregarious, independent, helpful and caring are more likely to receive support from others. Such information is of value to teachers designing remediation programmes. Sociolinguistic skills also contribute to the popularity of children among their peers (Gottman, 1986). The work of Pikas, (1989, in this volume), demonstrates the value of appropriate language in avoiding conflict. Gottman (1986) illustrates how language plays an important role in the formation and development of relationships. There are now many materials available for use in schools to facilitate the skills of friendship and communication (Bowers, 1987, Masheder, 1986).

Victimology

Children at risk of being bullied need to develop simple strategies to help them avoid attack. There is a wide range of such strategies, for example, avoid being last in a changing room, leave valuable possessions at home, try not to display anger or distress when bullied as this may encourage the bullies to continue. As adults we may have learnt to cope with threat and to avoid situations and company where we do not feel at ease. Some children may need to be instructed in routine safety procedures (for example, Elliott in this volume). There are a few critical seconds when voice, posture and display of confidence can tip the balance between attack and non attack so that by instructing the less confident children on how to behave under threat we may be offering them greater protection. Sadly some children may always be vulnerable to attack due to physique, race, poor co-ordination, speech or language difficulties or physical features. Knowing how to avoid and cope with provocation and attack must be part of any programme of work designed to support these children. Most people face provocation, to some degree, throughout their lives. How we respond determines whether or not the bullies elect to continue the attacks. We cannot expect vulnerable children to cope unless we have taught them the appropriate techniques.

Conclusion

In summary, we need to confront children with the fact that in a non-ideal world they will meet dominance and aggression in a variety of guises throughout their lives. As adults we can prepare them to be aware of high risk times and situations but we cannot protect them at all times unless they are under threat. By building up the confidence of vulnerable children, and by offering an appropriate code of conduct and interaction to the aggressors, we may better equip them for their future.

References

Besag, V. E. (1989) Bullies and Victims. Open University Press.

Bowers, S. (1987) Ways and Means: An Approach to Problem Solving, available from Quaker Meeting House, 76 Eden Street, Kingston on Thames KT1 1DJ.

Cowen, E. et al., (1973) Long Term follow up of early detected vulnerable children. Journal of Consultancy & Clinical Psychology 41, 438–46.

Dewey, J. (1916) Democracy in Education.

Elliott, M. (1986) unpublished research – personal communication. The Kidscape Project. Kidscape, 82 Brock Street, London W1Y 1YP.

Gottman, J. H. Parker, J. (eds.) (1986) Conversations of Friends: Speculations on Affective Development. Cambridge University Press.

Kohlberg, L. (1981) The Philosophy of Moral Development: Essays in Moral Development. (Vol. 1). New York: Harper Row.

Lane D. A. (1988) Violent histories: bullying and criminality in Tattum D. P. and Lane D. A. Bullying in Schools. Trentham Books, Stoke on Trent.

Masheder, M. (1986) Let's Cooperate. London Lithosphere Printing Corporation.

Measor, L. and Woods, P. (1984) Changing Schools: pupil perspectives on transfer to a secondary school. London: Open University Press.

Mortimore, P. et al., (1988) School Matters. The Junior Years. Somerset: Open Books Publishing Ltd.

Olweus, D. (1978) Aggression in Schools: Bullies & Whipping Boys. Wiley & Sons.

Olweus, D. (1980) Familial and Temperamental Determinants of Aggressive Behaviour in Adolescent Boys: A Causal Analysis, Developmental Psychology, Vol. 16, No. 6, pp. 644–660.

Olweus, D. (1987) Personal Communication, Also – Bully and Victim, problems

90

among school children in Scandinavia, in Myklebust, J. P. and Ommundson R. (eds.) PsykologproFesjonen mot ar 2060 Oslo Universitetsforlaget.

Roland, E. (1988) Bullying: the Scandinavian Research Tradition, in Tattum, D. P. and Lane D. A. Bullying in Schools. Trentham Books, Stoke on Trent.

Shrief E. (1986) talk given at F. I. R. M. Conference. Conflict in Schools Problem Solving and Mediation Skills.

CHAPTER 8

The Common Concern Method for the Treatment of Mobbing

Anatol Pikas

The waxing and waning of the Scandinavian – and especially Swedish – public interest in the phenomenon of mobbing is likely to be of interest to the rest of the world for two different reasons:

(1) It reflects some free-floating anxiety in a society which tries to combine the best of collectivistic and individualistic ideals.

(2) It reveals the hesitance of the teachers in such a society to treat decisively groups which are recognized as assaulting individual victims.

The best way to understand the cultural and psychological dynamics of the above is to follow attempts to treat mobbing in practice. Before we can do this, though, we must first discuss the use of the word mobbing itself.

Some investigators differentiate between 'mobbing' and 'bullying' while others don't

'Bullying' is a well-known concept in English derived from the word 'bully', designating a top dog who exerts oppressive, mostly physically violent behaviour on one or more persons. The noun bullying or the verb to bully may designate both of the following relationships:

* A single bully attacking an individual or group.

* A gang of bullies (sometimes with a leader, sometimes without a leader) attacking an individual or group.

The word mobbing however, designates only the second relationship –

in accordance with its original definition. Furthermore, because of practical considerations which will be explained later in this article, the word mobbing should be used only in this sense. That is to say, mobbing designates group violence.

It is possible that the word 'mobbing' has been used in social-psychological contexts for several centuries; however the best-known instance of it in modern times is in the writings of Konrad Lorenz who used it to designate an attack by a group of animals on an intruder (e.g. a flock of small birds attacking a crow or squirrel who plunders their nest). The word is still used in this way in the study of animal behaviour: mobbing is an attack by a group on a victim (or on an intruder who becomes a victim).

The concept was transferred from the animal to the human sphere by the Swedish surgeon Peter-Paul Heinemann, in several articles in the late 1960's and in a book in Swedish in 1972 which immediately became a best-seller and was translated into other Scandinavian languages. (Heinemann 1972.) However, the destiny of popular words is to become overused. Children and even adults started to use the word 'mobbing' to designate all kinds of attacking, even those where only one person (the bully or alleged bully) attacked the victim (or alleged victim). It also happened that a social scientist, Dan Olweus started to use the word differently from Heinemann's original definition. At about the same time as Heinemann was writing about mobbing, Olweus was carrying out investigations on 'Bullies and Whipping Boys' – a very appropriate title which he himself used of his work. It dealt with the subject without distinguishing between bullying carried out by a single person and bullying carried out by a group.

Again, in his later Swedish and Norwegian investigations giving figures on teachers' and students' estimations of violence among school children, Olweus labeled his investigation with the word mobbing without differentiating between the violence exerted by a single bully and that exerted by a group. As a result of this it is the case in Scandinavia that some scientists use the term 'mobbing' in the Heinemann's original sense (that is, to designate group violence only) while others, like Olweus, use the word as a synonym for 'bullying', indicating both group violence and individual violence.

The reason why the word 'mobbing' should be reserved for group violence

In a way, it would be convenient to say that no matter how a word is used, the only important thing is that the user describes his use of it. However, in the case of mobbing there is an important reason for reserving the new word mobbing for group violence – at least in social science – letting other kinds of violence be designated by other well established words like 'fight', 'conflict', 'controversy', 'harassment', and so on – as well as by the word 'bullying'.

The reason for reserving the word 'mobbing' only for group violence is that group violence has important characteristics which become decisive in treatment.

First of all, when one starts to treat mobbing, one meets up with the fact that the thoughts and feelings of a group are simpler than those of any of its individual members. All the members of a group strive towards a 'common psychological denominator' which is at the core of group dynamics.

Because of the relative simplicity of the 'collective mind', the behaviour of a group is predictable, and can thus be directed by a therapist who can combine a knowledge of this predictability with a certain amount of initiative and will. The most decisive and predictable factor in a mobbing group is that its members as individuals are themselves scared of their common denominator: they are caught up with the idea of tormenting a victim.

From this we can clearly derive the first important step for treatment: to re-individualize the group members through separate talks where their inherent fears and reservations towards their own mobbing behaviour are made conscious and an immediate escape from the noxious habit of mobbing is offered.

The background of the Common Concern method (CCm) for treatment

I have not, however, derived the above mentioned guide-line merely from deductive reasoning: the mobber's own deep desires to get rid of mobbing I discovered while curing the first cases in 1974. The situation at the time was that Heinemann's alarming publications had elicited much talk in Sweden about mobbing, nearly every contribution to the topic leading to an expression of the desire that 'something should be done about it'. The National Parent Association and private developers produced materials for discussion and for the mobilization of attitudes against mobbing. However, not much was done to deal with those actual cases of mobbing which had already developed to such a point that the outrage of a concerned public had no effect on the mobbers.

The first vague attempts made by school psychologists to treat mobbing failed. According to my view, these failures depended on the fact that the therapy was carried out with the entire mobbing group present together. My first attempts to treat the individual group members in a series of separate talks following certain principles met with immediate success. The reasons for it were described in a book (Pikas 1975) and the method which I used I today identify as the 'Suggestive Command method' (SCm). The reason for this name is that the therapeutic effect depends on the persuasive suggestions which the therapist gives to the individual. This method I still consider applicable in cases where the authority of the therapist is strong; in other words, in cases where the children are young (no older than about 12).

Later I developed a new method which can apparently be used with all cases of mobbing. It is called the Common Concern method (CCm) for the treatment of mobbing, described in a book published in Swedish. (Pikas 1987.) The book also describes the dynamics of mobbing as they are revealed in the treatment process; analyses various methods for prevention; describes several case histories of treatment; and relates my experiences in teaching the method to school teachers, indicating the most common failures among beginners.

It is not possible to give a summary of all the aspects of mobbing discovered during the treatment of numerous cases and elaborated in a book of 320 pages. What I consider would be the most useful to my present audience would be a simple summary of the basic guidelines of the Common Concern method (CCm).

The Common Concern method (CCm) for individual mobbers

According to this method, the therapeutic talks should begin with those students who are suspected of being mobbers. These individual talks, with about 3 to 6 suspected mobbers, should be carried out in a consecutive series with 10–20 minutes allotted for each talk – i.e. about 60–90 minutes in all. Immediately after this series is completed, we talk with the victim. After about a week, the talks are either repeated with the individuals or with those involved assembled as a group. The group talks may or may not include the victim, depending on the circumstances revealed during the first talks.

The reason for beginning with those who are suspected for mobbing is to protect the victim from being accused by the mobbers of having 'told on' them. Also, in preventive work, no enquiries about mobbing should be made among students. As soon as there is some evidence, usually obtained by adult observers, that mobbing may occur, the combined process of investigation and therapy begins.

The psychological process of therapy is summarized in figure 8.1. The vertical axis ranges from 'Communication on equal terms between the therapist and the student suspected of mobbing' to 'Strong experiences of common concern about tormenting the victim'.

The therapeutic dialogue can be summarized by five points on the scale, characterized by the following statements by the therapist:

1. 'I would like to talk with you because I've heard that you've been mean towards Kent.'
2. 'What do you know about it?'
3. 'All right, we've talked about it long enough.'
4. 'What to do? .... What do you suggest?'
5. 'That's good. We shall meet again in a week; then you can tell me how you've been getting on.'

Figure 8.1: The curve of emotional contact according to the Common-Concern-method (CCM)

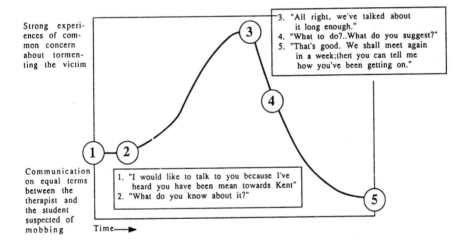

The most important step in the method is that between the second and the third point. Beginners often believe that at the second point the suspected mobber would answer with 'Nothing!' (or a similar expression). In fact, most mobbers want to talk about the situation. The task for the therapist, then, is to reinforce the mobber's answers with comments and further questions in such a way that the dialogue works towards the predetermined goal: the situation of the victim is something to be concerned about.

Though the whole purpose of the talk is to arrive at a common feeling, the therapist should never express verbally the notion that 'we share a common problem'; this has to be conveyed through implication and non-verbal signals. The therapist's success depends on his/her own empathy with Kent's torment as well as on a constructive and active expectation that during the talks the (former) mobber will eventually come to feel the same empathy.

Practically all school psychologists understand immediately that the therapeutic situation here is quite removed from an interrogation intended to uncover or state the guilt of a suspected mobber. Many school-teachers, however, need to work more with their own thoughts and feelings in order to discover in practice how to express the guiding theme of common concern for the victim. This need for extra work on the part of teachers does not of course mean that teachers have less capacity of empathy; rather, it results from habits which they have developed in resolving cases of mischief where the guilt of the offender has to be rapidly and safely found and reprimands administered.

For some teachers, the road to the feeling of common concern is easy and direct, for others it requires more effort. The interesting thing is that working towards the goals of common concern brings about a general improvement in the teacher's ability to communicate with his/her students in other situations as well.

However, a good therapist is also prepared for those occasions where, despite his/her well-balanced nonverbal signals (do not overdo the friendliness!) the mobber may answer: 'I don't know anything!'. In this case, that therapist should not try to put forward the facts (or possible facts) in order to convince the subject of his participation in mobbing. This would lead to a dispute which the therapist would certainly win in regards to the truth – but still more certainly lose in regards to the development of a partnership between therapist and subject necessary for the victim's rehabilitation.

When it happens that the mobber denies knowledge of the case, one must so to speak, take 'two steps back', and start to talk in a relaxed manner about the social environment of the class and at length come closer to the victim's situation. Beginners should then watch for even the slightest signs of admittance on the part of the mobber that the situation of the victim is not good, and reinforce such admittance delicately. This requires time and practice, but if the aspiring therapist is prepared to make a serious effort to learn how, he will find specific examples of it in my book on mobbing treatment.

We have so far implied that the person who is mobbed is an innocent victim (in accordance with Heinemann's description, repeated later in numerous newspaper articles). In our method, though, this innocence should be considered no more than a first hypothesis, which we try to verify in our talks with the mobber without pushing too hard. If, however, the suspected mobber says that the alleged victim himself is a bully and gives spontaneous examples of this, we should be prepared to test such a statement by the mobber as a second hypothesis.

At this point a beginner often asks:

- How does one know what the truth is?

To which I respond in my courses with:

- Tell me first, what shall we do with the truth in this case?

Sooner or later we arrive at the common conclusion that unless one does not intend to punish but merely to cure the mobbing, then it is not necessary to know the truth behind who is guilty if that truth is difficult to uncover. What we are attempting is to reach with the former mobber a common experience of concern for the present state of affairs. Even if the subject is without guilt, the therapist would expect that as a decent human being he/she would be worried about the situation as such.

As soon as the therapist and the suspected mobber have encountered the problem together, the time has come for the therapist to leave off examining the situation further and introduce the way towards a constructive outcome.

This happens at points 3 and 4. Often the questions suggested at point 4 create a turning point ('What to do? .... What do you suggest?') Sometimes if talking about the situation has been too taxing, the therapist needs to say the lines in point 3 ('All right, we've talked about it long enough.') in order to create the optimal reception for the decisive lines in point 4. The previous talks have served as a preparation for this: what can we as partners do together?

Here the creative activity starts. Our tension curve slides down towards the level 'communication on equal terms'.

Beginners are often astonished to find that mobbers (or alleged mobbers) so often have adequate suggestions about improving the situation of the victim, or if not, at least promise to stop mobbing. The explanation for this is evident. Participation in mobbing has created an emotional arousal but instead of getting punished, the emotional arousal is given a constructive outlet.

But still, the new relationship between the therapist and the former mobber needs to be reinforced. So the therapist says his line according to our final point, numbered 5.

After this talk, the 'partners' say goodbye and the next student suspected of being a mobber is asked to enter. When the therapeutic discussions with a selected group of suspected mobbers are finished, then it is time to talk with the victim (or the alleged victim).

Talks with the victim

The tension curve of the emotional contact with the victim is quite different from that of the suspected mobbers. As shown in figure number 8.2, the meeting starts from the point 'on equal terms'. That is, the therapist simply says:

> - How are you?

When the student has the main characteristics of the classic innocent victim, the curve remains largely 'within the victim's playground'. If, however, the victim turns out to be a teaser, or even a bully, the talks are on the therapist's 'playground'.

We first follow the therapy with the classical victim and call him, for the sake of brevity, 'Kent'.

In the beginning, the therapist is just supportive, reinforcing everything Kent has to say. Actually, I and my collaborators have hardly ever met a victim who is reluctant to talk. The victims talk with relief and even pleasure. We have never met a victim in the regular therapy who is scared that the alleged mobbers will seek revenge for his having 'ratted' on them. While the method was in the developmental stage we made special investigations in order to discover the reasons for the victim's openness towards the therapist. We found that the former mobbers, when they returned to the classroom, had non-verbally transmitted their relief to the others and had in this way quite delicately and unconsciously announced to the victim that a change had occurred in their relationship.

Certainly, it could be that Kent has a weakling's behaviour because of the mobbing, but also the opposite may be valid: his fear for the fellows was the origin for his being mobbed. The main problem for the therapist now is: should I continue my supportive meetings with Kent alone or can I use the group of former mobbers as a therapy group for Kent acting around him without my absence?

Our curves in figure 8.2 are not normative as in figure 8.1; they are just typical examples of therapies which have occurred. We shall first follow Kent's therapy.

After the introductory session the therapist becomes convinced that the victim is really a classical one and starts a supportive therapy (which is, in reality longer than that indicated on the curve).

Figure 8.2: The classic victim and the provocative victim

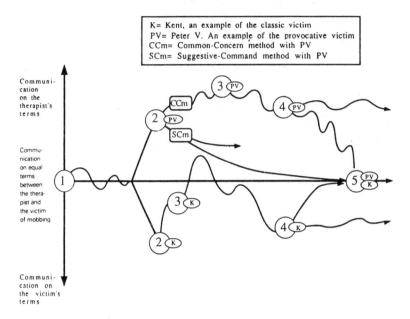

At point 2 the therapist starts to introduce Kent to the idea that he himself could do a lot to improve his situation.

At point 3 the therapist introduces the objective fact that a part of Kent's problem is that the others are disturbed by his unclean clothes, and he convinces Kent that a washing is necessary. In this part of the therapy, the therapist brings the interaction 'into his playground'. Later, the discussion returns again to Kent's 'playground'. At the point 4, the therapist has to decide whether he should continue the therapy only with Kent or whether he/she should go on to point 5, and have a meeting between Kent and the former mobbers.

A meeting with both the former victim and the former mobbers is the final goal of our method. Before we turn to that I shall explain the upper part of figure 8.2.

After the initial exploring session, the therapist discovers that the picture he has got from talks with the alleged mobbers is true: the person he is talking with is certainly a victim, but a provocative one. We shall call the provocative victim 'Peter V'.

The therapist now follows somewhat the same line as when he was talking with the mobbers: he seeks to share with Peter V the feeling that the situation is not good, and sooner or later they arrive to that conclusion. At this point, the realization that the group's persecution of him is partly dependent on his own behaviour also begins to appear in Peter

V. At point 2 the therapist has to decide whether (1) he should tell Peter V straight away that if he himself stops provoking the others, the others will stop provoking him, or whether (2) he should implant this idea in Peter V during a longer session.

In case of the former alternative, we follow a variant of the Suggestive Command method (SCm), which is possible only when the therapist's authority is strong. As with CCm the objective with CCm is to reach point 5: a meeting with the former mobbers.

Let us, however, continue along the milder CCm-road. The therapist continues to gain Peter V's confidence and begins to learn about his way of thinking. At point 3, the therapist discovers that Peter V is willing to discuss 'different ways to become popular.' This gives the therapist a good opportunity to introduce the idea that Peter V wants very much to become popular with 'the guys', but is going about it in the wrong way. The therapist and Peter V now discuss possibly more acceptable ways of reaching a more genuine popularity than that which Peter V has previously enjoyed.

At point 4 the therapist and Peter V reach the problem which prepares for the final point: can the mobbers accept Peter V's new way of approaching them? Can they change their prejudices and give Peter V another chance?

Certainly this would be something to find out through discussion. But such a discussion has to be prepared. The therapist says that he is going to meet the former mobbers, most probably as a group; if they are prepared to meet Peter V in a positive spirit, he will let him know.

The final group talks

There should be no exception to the rule that the therapist returns to meet the mobbers once again after about a week and talks about their success with and/or failure to help the victim. It is, however, dependent on the therapist's own intuitive decision whether these meetings should be carried out with individuals or in groups. Statistically speaking, when the victim is Peter V, the provocative victim, it is almost always necessary to arrange group meetings. We shall now deal with this case.

It rarely occurs that the talks with individuals have led to outcome so successful that the mobbers and the victim can meet together in a group after only a week. More often the therapist first meets the group of mobbers wihtout the victim.

This meeting starts with the therapist's question:

- How has the week gone?

The therapist then merely listens to what the former mobbers have to say. Normally, they begin with some rather superficial remarks about their contacts with the victim. Later, they enter into a phase where the blame put on the absent Peter V dominates. One should not immediately counter this with criticisms. Eventually, when everyone's difficulties have been aired, ask clearly the well-known questions:

- What shall we do! What do you suggest?

If the former mobbers still dwell on the blaming phase after this, listen awhile and then repeat the questions again, still more probingly. It has happened to me that I have had to repeat them with increasing emphasis four times before I received a direct response.

The general answer to these questions is that we can neither 'cure' nor 'convert' Peter V without having a decent and constructive meeting with him. Hence, what we should do is to prepare a meeting with him in such a way as to give the constructiveness the best chance.

- How shall we parepare ourselves? you ask the group.

Sooner or later you will propose the following plan. First, each of the former mobbers in turn will express, in sincere and positive terms, his opinion about Peter V who just listens. Then the therapist, as mediator, asks Peter V what he has to say about what he has just heard. It is likely that his answers will also be positive, in which case we have a good start. Of course, all the participants in the meeting eventually get the chance to air their problems with each other, but if we make a good start, we more easily find ways of living together.

I have never met with any objections from the former mobbers to such a plan. What we now have to do is to bring Peter V into the meeting.

It is best not to ask the (former) victim to participate in such a way that he has a chance to say 'no'. One should start instead in a more suggestive way like this:

- I have something very intersting to tell you . . . . I've just been talking with Jeff, Bob and Chris and they had some good things to say about you! Can you believe it? Come, let us go and listen. You don't need to say anything.

It requires a certain amount of enthusiasm and suggestiveness from the therapist to elicit enough curiosity in the former victim that he/she is willing to come and see with his/her own eyes and hear with his/her own ears what the former mobbers have to say. I have never failed in coaxing the former victim to the meeting because I have relied upon the natural curiosity of young people.

How well the meeting between the former victim and his/her former mobbers works out depends on how well we have prepared it in advance. Certainly, unexpected reproaches may occur from both sides: this only means that the session will take more time. Under the guidance of the therapist the parties involved will find a way of living together sooner or later.

Needless to say, the therapist is there first and foremost to facilitate communication. He/she should strictly avoid playing the role of judge, prosecutor or solicitor and instead maintain the position of an active mediator by giving as many positive, mainly nonverbal suggestions as possible and by ensuring that the students speak in a proper order. ('Oh, that was well put . . . . Jeff, what do you say when you hear such a nice remark from Peter V? . . . . Did you notice, Peter, what Chris was offering you just now?' And so on.)

When the parties involved have finally reconciled themselves, reinforce their good feelings about what they have decided. But before you end the meeting, be sure to bring up the following problem:

– What shall we do if somebody cannot keep the promises he's made?

Most often the students suggest a penalty for failure to comply. Tell them that this is not the best way because it encourages them to monitor each other's mistakes – at which point the accusations and conflicts re-surface again.

– Do you know what is meant by 'tolerance'?

Let the students explain the concept, and then present your conclusion: we must learn to tolerate each other's mistakes. You, Chris, Jeff and Bob must 'let Peter V live', and you, Peter, must allow the others to make (their) mistakes.

It has been my experience that kids understand this very well and remember what it means to 'let the other side live'.

Here, the mobbing therapy is ended. To be sure that progress is made the therapist tells the students that he/she will come back in a week or a month and see how they are doing.

Discovering the mechanisms governing interest in mobbing problems

There are two different ways for teachers to fight mobbing: one is to promote attitudes against mobbing in general, the other is to intrude therapeutically in actual cases. The first does not work when mobbing groups are well developed: the promotion of anti-mobbing attitudes does not reach those mobbers who have already developed a group cohesive-ness.

It is quite evident that in training teachers to become mobbing therapists there is a threshold between those teachers who prefer to engage the mobbers in close talks about their mobbing activities and those who are not happy with this role. A rough estimate based on experience in this field would put the numbers of those teachers who feel able to become therapists at around 10–15%. Once a teacher who belongs to this group has taken the first step towards starting treatment of mobbing he/she encounters few failures.

Those who have lifted the burden of mobbing from a victim find in their work a deep feeling of satisfaction.

The starting point for working with already existing mobbing groups is found when a small group of teachers at a school form a study-and-action-group. They read and discuss the literature on mobbing therapy (and not merely talks about the mechanisms and the occurrence of mobbing). They should begin to treat simple cases relating their experiences and results in seminars. It is of great advantage if the teachers work in cooperation with a school psychologist whom they know can take over treatment if for example a particular case requires individual treatment.

There can be difficulties if teachers do not treat actual cases of mobbing and instead rely entirely on campaigns by lectures showing movies and arranging role plays designed to promote anti-mobbing attitudes. This may have a good effect, if mobbers exist in the class, they might then be encouraged to regard their first attempts at mobbing as a rather exciting activity.

Teachers if they are to create attitudes against mobbing need to send clear signals that actual cases of mobbing will be tackled. Certainly, these signals must be trustworthy and *the best way to obtain trustworthiness is to treat actual cases.*

There is an immense need in Scandinavian, and especially Swedish society for dealing with mobbing on the verbal and emotional level. However, this need is not proportional to the willingness of that society to deal with those cases which actually occur.

Conclusion

My philosophy behind mobbing therapy is derived from the goal to learn to communicate in order to resolve conflicts. Its theoretical principles are expressed in the academic discipline of Communication Education for Conflict Resolutuon which I have been teaching at Uppsala University. Operationally this involves two programs: one constructed for students containing exercises for dealing with situations where 'conflict is in the air', and the other for teachers who have 'difficulties with discipline problems'. In implementing these programs I have discovered a general feature shared by those teachers who become involved in mobbing therapy.

This feature can be described as a person's discovery of the great adventure of communicating constructively with 'the other side' when conflicts are 'in the air'. 'The other side' takes many forms: students who do not follow the teacher's demand for discipline, a spouse in a marriage, a political opponent – or children mobbing a schoolmate.

It is not important from which direction a teacher begins to develop his/her ability to approach the other side constructively. To start meeting with the mobbers is one of the possible starting points. For those who choose this path I have observed a personal growth in practically all involved teachers – a growth which effects not only their teaching, but also their ability and willingness to deal constructively with people in general.

References

Heinemann, P.P. (1972). Mobbing – grippvåld. (Mobbing – Group Violence). Stockholm: Nature & Kultur.

Olweus, D. (1973). Hackkycklingar och översittare. Forskning om skolmobbning. (Whipping-boys and bullies) (Stockholm: Almqvist & Wiksell).

Olweus, D.(1988) Mobbning – grundläggande fakta och ett framgängsrikt åtgärdsprogram. (Mobbing – basic facts and a successful action programme) Stockholm: Psycholog Tidningen (In press).

Pikas, A. (1975) Så stoppar vi mobbning (So we stop mobbing in school) Stockholm: Prisma.

Pikas, A. (1988) Så bekampar vi mobbning i skolan (So we fight mobbing in school) Uppsal: Ama dataservice förlag.

Pikas, A. (1988) En mobbningsterapeuts syn. (A mobbing therapist's view) Stockholm: *Psykolog Tidningen* (In press).

CHAPTER 9

Bullying – Harmless Fun or Murder?

Michele Elliott

In January 1988 twelve year old John was on his way home in London from a friend's house, an older bully approached him and demanded money. John replied that he didn't have any. The youth pulled a knife. 'Don't mess around. Give me your money.' John knew he had to do something; he didn't have any money and he was very frightened. Suddenly John yelled a deep, loud yell, which startled the youth. As he yelled, John started running towards his house. He pounded on the door and rang the bell. He told his mother what had happened and then started shaking. She looked out, but the youth had disappeared.

John's mother gave her son a piece of paper so he could write down the details and immediately rang the police. When they had finished questioning him, they complimented John on his clear thinking. John replied that he had been 'kidscaped, so he knew what to do'. He had learned the strategies which helped him to deal with a potentially deadly situation. Some children are not so lucky.

In 1988, 12 year old John Griffin of Kent nearly died of alcohol poisoning after being forced to drink three quarters of a bottle of whiskey by a 23 year old bully.

In Spetember 1986, 13 year old Ahmed Iqbal Ullah of Manchester died from a stab wound trying to defend a friend from a bully. (Grice, 1988) On September 25, 1985, Mark Providence Perry of Oxon died. He had been the victim of sustained bullying. As he cycled past the place he had been ambushed and attacked by bullies the day before, he accelerated right into the path of a van and was killed. Mark's teacher reported that he had been pushed and ostracized in the lesson and was distressed. As he left school, he was again harassed by having his bicycle hidden under a pile of bikes. Witnesses say he was looking backwards towards the school and not at the van when he was hit. Extreme examples of the bullying problem facing many children or isolated incidents?

The Kidscape primary school research

In a study conducted with 4000 children from 1984 to 1986 Elliott (1986), I found that 65% of the children complained about being bullied. 1520 of the children (38%) had experienced either a particularly frightening incident or had been bullied at least twice or more. Of the children who were bullied, 1033 were boys (68%) of the victims and 483 were girls (32%) of the victims. Of the boy victims 121, and of the girls victims 30, seemed to be chronically and severely bullied to the point that it was affecting their everyday lives. Some of these children were terrified to go to school and were often truant or ill. It would seem that bullying is one of the most common problems of children.

In this same study, when the parents of the children were asked how they coped with bullying, only 4% had tried to intervene to stop the bullying. Although many expressed concern, the reasons for not getting involved ranged from: 'it's an age old problem – always happened, always will' to 'let the kids sort it out' and 'just hit back.'

Yet those children who are bullied are often the ones who cannot fight back or who do not wish to fight. Mark's mother, a teacher, says 'My son was an unaggressive studious boy whose life was made a misery by suffering daily harrassment and violent bullying at school. He tried all possible ways to cope with it and to control his panic. But the bullying got worse because staff took no effective action. Mark sometimes tried to stick up for himself on advice from teachers, but that only served to get him into trouble for defending himself.'

In my experience in dealing with the victims of bullying, when children such as Mark lash out in panic or retaliate, it often just fuels the bully's vindictiveness. Bullies are far more cunning than their victims and it is the victim who gets caught out. Sometimes the victims get labeled as 'trouble makers' for trying to defend themselves.

We know that the victims of bullying suffer real torment. They become frightened of going to school, have nightmares, feel humiliated, and even have nervous breakdowns or attempt suicide. (Campbell, 1988).

One 12 year old wrote to KIDSCAPE:

I have been picked on since I started school. Three girls always bother me because I talk different to them. They say I have to pay them 10p everyday or they will turn everyone against me. I cry myself to sleep every night. Now everyone else won't speak to me and I am hated. I keep breaking into tears which makes it all worse. I want friends and need help. Can you tell me what to do?

Another wrote:

There is a girl at my school who bullies everyone, but me especially. She writes things on my books, yells at me and follows me home. I don't want to go to school and try to get my mum to let me stay home but she won't. Last week I took a lot of aspirin – I thought it would kill me but it just made me sick. I didn't tell my mum why I was sick, but I didn't have to go to school that day.

My mum say that this girl is just jealous of me, but that doesn't help. I feel that there is no hope because nothing will change, no one wants to know.

Bullying takes many forms – verbal abuse, emotional badgering, physical attack, sexual harrassment. It may be a one off incident with a random victim or a campaign against a particular person. The bully can be another child, a gang, or an adult such as a parent or teacher. (Elliott, 1988a).

Why do children become bullies?

It may be a temporary response to a change in their lives such as a divorce, the birth of a baby, the death of someone they love, moving, going to a new school. This type of bullying is worrying, but can usually be sorted out by helping the child come to terms with the cause. It is much more difficult to deal with chronic bullies. Most often they have themselves been abused or bullied. They grow up feeling insecure, inadequate, humiliated, and stupid. As children they were not allowed to show feelings of tenderness or be weak in anyway, were put under pressure to succeed, but never complimented of felt a sense of accomplishment.

Why children become chronic bullies

In growing up, these children have often:

- Felt insecure, humiliated, inadequate
- Been bullied by parents or siblings
- Been made the scapegoat in the family
- Been physically, emotionally or sexually abused
- Not been allowed to show feelings
- Been subjected to enormous pressure to succeed

- Felt different to their peers
- Felt no sense of accomplishment

(Moore, 1987)

Adult bullies describe being unfairly punished from a young age for things they could not help, like accidentally wetting the bed or spilling food or falling over. The adult has an impossible expectation of the child and makes it clear that being dependent or vulnerable are not acceptable. Being outwardly 'strong' and humiliating others are acceptable. Inwardly, bullies may be emotionally insecure. They may need counselling, but bullying behaviour is difficult to change because the underlying motive is often self hatred brought on by years of being made to feel small and inadequate.

Instead of facing the possibility that it might be their problem, bullies use any excuse to lash out at others. The bullies with whom I have worked often say the victim deserves to be bullied because he or she is different in some way. So the victim is picked on because of race, religion, looks, intelligence, slowness, being clumsy or talented, having a disfigurement, talking with a different accent – the list is endless. The only common criteria is that the bullying continues as long as the victim cannot cope or until someone steps in to help.

What can be done?

Sometimes children have to do what a bully or older person tells them because they are frightened or just don't know what to do. One little boy had his bicycle taken from him in the park by an older, stronger bully. He was so scared of getting into trouble for losing his bike, that he fought the bully and ended up with severe injuries.

Mark's mother, Janet Perry, says: 'teach children that their safety is the most important consideration. Children should not feel that they have to fight to protect possessions, nor that hitting back at the bully will necessarily solve the problem.' Adults need to be willing to intervene in these situations and not turn their backs or claim that bullying is just one of the things children have to put up with. Sometimes it helps to get a group of children together and have them say no together to the bully. As Linda Frost, headmistress of Montem Junior School in London says: 'We have a responsibility to help children deal with bullies – it should be unacceptable behaviour to both adults and to other children. We have dealt with bullies using the Kidscape programme involving the children so that the bullying of ANY child is not on – the other children won't allow it. Also parents and teachers must give support because it is unfair to expect children to deal with it alone.'

Valerie Besag, (Besag, 1989) has argued that:

> 'Children who are bullied lack confidence, so teaching them the assertive exercises like those in the Kidscape programme, could be very helpful. Also, supervision of groups of children is vital, as most bullying occurs out of sight. Supervision can eliminate bullying in schools, for example.'

In the UK the KIDSCAPE programmes in schools for 3 to 5 year olds and 6 to 11 year olds are designed to protect children from a variety of dangers, including bullying, abduction, getting lost and possible sexual abuse. The programmes are now in use with over 600,000 children. The problem of bullying is dealt with by involving the parents, teachers and children in discussions and roleplaying positive strategies to deal with bullying. There are also stories to be read to the children. Following the lessons the children make up their own roleplays and stories.

The Kidscape programme starts with children as young as 3 to 5, as well as children with special needs such as mental handicaps. The Under Fives programme is simply worded and gives one message per lesson. It has also been used with older children for whom English is a second language. The programme includes roleplays for use with puppets, dolls or to be played out by the teachers and the children.

Before and after being involved in the roleplays and/or stories, the children will have had discussion about bullying, getting lost, not going with strangers, touching or whatever issue is in the lesson.

As an example of a story for the younger children, KIDSCAPE has given permission for the following story excerpts about bullying to be printed from the Under Fives Manual (Elliott, 1988b):

The Bully – Part One

It was a very cold day. Petunia wanted to go out to play on the swings, so she dressed up nice and warm. First she put on her woolly jumper. Then she put on her coat, which she could do up all by herself. She was the first one on the playground. She quickly went over to the swing and got on.

Her older sister taught her how to get the swing started by pushing herself. Soon Petunia was swinging high in the air.

'This is really fun,' she thought.

The other children were coming on the playground now. There was her friend Diane.

'Hi, Diane,' shouted Petunia, 'look at me!'

Diane waved and came over to the swings. She was careful not to get too close to the swing that Petunia was on. She didn't want to get hit by the swing or by Petunia's feet!

All the children were playing now. Some were on the swings, some were playing tag and Dee Dee and John had climbed right to the top of the climbing frame. Petunia thought they were very brave – she didn't like climbing very much.

Some other children were coming onto the playground now. One of the children came straight over to Petunia and said:

'Get off – I want to swing!'

Petunia was a little frightened. 'But I only just got on,' she said.

'I don't care. I said I want a turn – MOVE!'

'But that's not fair,' said Petunia. 'I'll give you a go in a minute.'

The bully grabbed the swing and shouted 'GET OFF!'

Petunia fell down and began to cry.

The bully said: 'Now you go away and you better not tell. Only babies tell tales. You promise not to tell?'

Petunia was very unhappy. It wasn't fair. But the bully looked so mean that Petunia said 'I promise.'

What should Petunia do?

The Bully – Part Two

Petunia didn't tell anyone what happened. She felt very sad about how mean the bully had been to her. But Petunia didn't know what to do. Her friend Diane got off the swing and came over to Petunia.

'What's wrong?' said Diane.

'That bully pushed me off the swing,' sniffed Petunia.

'Tell the teacher,' said Diane.

'I can't,' said Petunia.

'Why not?'

'I promised I wouldn't.'

'I think you should tell,' said Diane.

'No, let's just go and play with that ball,' said Petunia.

Petunia and Diane began playing with the ball.

Petunia was feeling better now. Just then, the bully came over to where they were playing.

'Give me the ball,' said the bully.

Petunia and Diane looked at each other. What should they do? (You may wish to ask the children here)

Petunia reached for Diane's hand. She felt braver holding hands.

'GIVE ME THE BALL!' shouted the bully.

'No!' said Petunia in a loud voice.

'No!' said Diane. 'We're playing with the ball.'

The bully looked really mean. 'GIVE ME THE BALL. NOW!'

'NO!' shouted Petunia and Diane together. 'Let's tell the teacher' whispered Diane to Petunia. The children turned to go find their teacher.

'I don't want the ball anyway,' said the bully. 'You're just a couple of babies.'
Petunia and Diane felt happy. Petunia knew she couldn't keep a promise to the bully because it wasn't a fair promise. Diane had helped her friend, Petunia, and Diane felt good.
How about the bully?
Well, the bully was not very happy. It is not nice to be a bully. The bully didn't have any friends. How could the bully get some friends?

In dealing with children aged 5 to 11, stories and roleplays are also used, with discussion before and after. The following excerpt is reproduced from the Kidscape Primary Kit (Elliott, 1986) with permission:

'Now we are going to act out a little play. It's about a child called Alice. (If there is a child in the class called Alice, remember to change the name!) The play starts with a girl called Lucy throwing a ball against a wall in the school playground. While you are watching, think about what you would do if this happened to you.'

N.B. If you have decided to read the story instead of doing the roleplay, turn to page 4 in the Storybook.

Roleplay 1 – The playground bully

(Lucy is playing with a tennis ball: throwing it against a wall and catching it. Alice is watching her from a distance)

Lucy One.... two.... three.... four....
Alice Hi, Lucy. Give us a catch then.
Lucy Hold on a minute. I'm in the middle of something. Eight.... nine....
Alice (Snatching the ball out of Lucy's hands as she is about to catch the ball) Look at that! Brilliant! What a catch!
Lucy Oi! Hold on....
Alice I said give us a catch, didn't I?
Lucy I was going to....
Alice Well, that's all right then, innit? Come on then, catch this! (She throws the ball quite hard at Lucy).
Lucy (Dropping the ball) Hey, not so hard!
Alice Stop wingeing and throw me the ball.
Lucy I don't want to play any more.
Alice (Sternly) Throw me the ball, Lucy!
Lucy I've got to go home. Honest
Alice Too bad. We're playing catch. Throw me the ball
Lucy Oh come on Alice, please. I've got to go.
(Alice goes to Lucy and snatches the ball out of her hands).

Alice   Look, Lucy, don't mess me around, all right?
(She throws Lucy the ball, softer than before. Lucy catches it).
Alice   OK. Now give me a catch.
(Reluctantly, Lucy throws Alice the ball).
End

'Now we are going to act out the second part of this little play. Let's see what Lucy does on the next day. This time, Lucy is playing with a friend called Claire.' (If you use the stories instead of the roleplays, stop the story at an appropriate point so that the children can practise shouting 'no' again).

Roleplay 2 – the playground bully

(Lucy is playing catch with her friend Claire)

Lucy   It was horrible! She just wouldn't let me go. I was really late. My mum was livid. And I couldn't tell her why – I didn't dare. She said she was going to come back today too. I hate her! (They carry on throwing the ball to each other).

Lucy   Twenty eight . . . . twenty nine . . . . Listen, Claire. If she comes up today, don't leave me, right?

Claire   All right.

Lucy   We'll just keep on playing, yeah. Maybe she'll go away if there's two of us. We could just tell her we don't want to play with her.

Claire   OK. Maybe she won't come anyway. Thirty one . . . . thirty two . . . . (Alice appears at a distance)

Alice   Oi! Lucy! Give us a catch then! You clear off, Claire! Come on, Lucy! Let's see how far you can throw the ball!

Lucy   (To Claire) You stick around, right! You promised, remember.

Claire   Sure.

Alice   Come on. Don't mess me about. Throw me the ball!

Lucy   No, I won't Alice. Just leave us alone. I'm playing with Claire.

Alice   Not any more you're not. You're playing with me! Bye-bye, Claire.

Lucy
&
Claire   No! You clear off. Leave us alone. We don't want to play with you!

Alice   Oh you don't, huh! Well, too –

Lucy   No we don't. And if you don't leave us alone, I'll tell my mum. And I'll tell her why I was so late home the other day too.

Claire   Yeah, and I'll tell my big brother.

Alice   Oh shut up. Both of you! I don't want to play your rotten game anyway. Ya pair of big babies. (Alice leaves. Claire and Lucy laugh and carry on playing)

End

Points to stress

> Tell someone
> Ask a friend to help you
> You can say 'NO'

The children and teachers also discuss why children are bullies and what can be done to help them. There has been considerable success in stopping school bullying by peer pressure through the KIDSCAPE programme. However, changing the behaviour and dealing with the problem bully has been more difficult. In some cases we have found that the bully stops the behaviour at school, but continues it in another environment. Long term counselling is often needed for the bully and the family, but it is usually not available. This is one area which needs more research.

Conclusion

There will always be those who say there is nothing at all can be done about the problem of bullying. But Stephenson and Smith (1988) in their study on bullying in North-East England, found that bullying was frequently more of a problem in some schools than others. This would seem to indicate that the attitude towards the problem is crucial. If bullying is allowed, it will go on as Lane (1988) has argued.

The final word I leave to Mark's mother:

> 'For three years Mark attended a school where he was never bullied, so I know it is possible to eradicate bullying. No child should have to endure what Mark went through. Bullying can and must always be stopped and not by the victim, but by the adults. When the bullying is going on at school, it should be dealt with by the teachers and involve the parents. If the Kidscape principles had been used by my son's school, he would still be alive today.'

For a copy of the Kidscape Code and information about schools programmes, send a large sae to:

Kidscape
82 Brook Street
London W1Y 1YG

114

References

Grice, E. (1988) Race: The Fatal Flaw, Sunday Times, 1 May 1988, Section B.

Elliott, M. (1986) KIDSCAPE Primary Kit. London, Kidscape.

Campbell, C. (1988) Bully For You, Just Seventeen. July, pages 26–27.

Elliott, M. (1988) Keeping Safe, A Practical Guide to Talking with Children. London, Hodder & Stoughton.

Besag, V. (1989) Bullies and Victims. London, Open University Press.

Elliott. M. (1988) Kidscape Under Five's Programme. London, Kidscape.

Elliott, M. (1986) Kidscape Primary Kit. London, Kidscape.

Lane, D.A. (1988) Violent histories, bullying and criminality: in Tattum, D.P. and Lane, D.A. (1988) Bullying in Schools. Professional Development Foundation, Trentham Books.

Moore, M. (1987) Report of the European Teachers' Seminar on 'Bullying in Schools', Strasbourg, Council of Europe.

Stephenson, P. and Smith, D. (1988) Bullying in the Primary School: in Tattum, D.P. and Lane, D.A. (1988) Bullying in Schools. Professional Development Foundation, Trentham Books.

CHAPTER 10

Some Practical Approaches to Bullying

Simon Priest

> 'Very well then, let's roast him,' cried Flashman, and catches hold of
> Tom by the collar; one or two boys hesitate, but the rest join in.
>
> *Tom Brown's Schooldays by Thomas Hughes*

Background

As an Educational Psychologist working for a British LEA I periodically
encounter concerns about bullying on my regular visits to schools. What
seems to distinguish this issue from other aspects of my work is the
absence of any shared conceptual framework or useful knowledge-base.
As a result, the professionals involved are obliged to deal with each new
situation on the basis of their own professional experience. There are no
validated approaches and no obvious ways of sharing successful practice.

Whilst this has immediate implications for teachers engaged in
pastoral care in schools it also has ramifications for educational psychologists who may find themselves less able to operate in their newly
emerging role of 'consultants'. Instead they may be drawn in to casework
which is often repetitive and which may not be the best use of allocation
of their time available for that school. What is more, there is a growing
acceptance amongst teachers and other related professionals that 'ownership' of a child's difficulties should, wherever possible, remain with the
school and that the proper function of outside agencies and support
services is to enable this to happen. It is less easy to offer practical advice
and support where bullying is concerned due to the lack of methodology
and useful literature.

As a result of these and other considerations I became interested in exploring what educational psychology had got to offer staff faced with the
responsibility of dealing with bullying at first hand.

Around this time I was asked to take part in a series of house meetings involving all the boys at a local Special School for youngsters with emotional and behavioural problems. In this setting, as might be imagined, disagreement, conflict and bullying are potentially regular features of school life. This is especially exacerbated by the fact that those boys with the least personal difficulties soon return home and to mainstream schools leaving behind the least socially skilled. As a result there is an absence of mature and competent role models to guide the younger boys. At the outset of the first of three open-discussion sessions there was an initial phase of awkwardness and embarrassment but thereafter I was struck by the power of the feelings expressed by the boys about their own and each others antisocial behaviour. Whilst a number of practical interventions were considered (such as inter-dormitory competitions, a commendation book or an 'anti-bully squad') the most important aspect seemed to be the therapeutic nature of the sessions. These gave many of the youngsters an opportunity to express their own distress but equally important to learn how their behaviour impinged on their schoolmates. The need for personal catharsis was obvious but equally important was the value of helping youngsters to provide each other with honest and immediate feedback about their behaviour.

What follows is not a theoretical dissertation but a review of some practical approaches to bullying in this locality over the last 18 months.

Surveying Pupils

In the area where I work many secondary schools are becoming increasingly sophisticated in surveying the attitudes and perceptions of staff and students as part of the process of evaluating their institution's needs and planning their own 'in-house' approaches to the problems identified. Where these surveys include questions about bullying as part of a broad range of questions they invariably tend to bear out the impression of the teachers who do not see bullying as a problem for the vast majority of their children. There is, at the same time, a very real concern in schools that there should not be an over-emphasis on bullying which might lead to unrealistic levels of worry and a lack of confidence. This type of effect has been reported as a result of the publicity for some of the Neighbourhood Watch schemes encouraged by the police and directed towards community involvement in reducing crime.

There is considerable anecdotal evidence from talking with teachers and children which suggests that children's anxiety about bullying peaks immediately prior to a change of school, phase or site. The pastoral staff in schools responsible for liaising with their primary feeder schools are particularly familiar with this. One local secondary school addressed this issue directly in the course of a longitudinal survey of changing perceptions as a cohort of children moved from the second to the third year which also involved a transition from Lower School to Upper School site. In this unpublished study, undertaken by one of the form tutors, it was found that anticipated bullying was the most common concern of the second year children prior to their transfer, but in the vast majority of cases their fears had been unwarranted and they subsequently reported no such problems. These data and those from surveys of parents suggest a need for delicate balance between identifying the very real but relatively infrequent episodes of bullying and on the other hand reassuring children and parents, especially at known 'high anxiety' times.

In a different context a pupil-survey was used as part of the response of a pastoral team (Year Head, Form Tutor, Educational Welfare Officer, School Matron and Educational Psychologist) in a local secondary school to a specific allegation of bullying. Although the complainant was clearly distressed to the extent of refusing to attend school, there was no firm evidence against the alleged bully whose intimidation was said to be verbal rather than physical. Given the suspicion that this pupil may have been involved in upsetting other children and in an attempt to examine whether bullying was a more widespread problem, it was decided to take the unusual step of surveying the entirety of the third and fourth year pupils, aged 14 and 15 years, a total of some 340 children.

A short questionnaire was devised with the bullying item being innocuously 'embedded' between a similarly structured question about school meals and another about choices of subject options in the fourth year. The question paper was delivered without prior notification or discussion to the whole of the two year groups one Monday morning and completed anonymously. In answer to the question, 'Are you being bullied?', around 80 per cent of the children ticked the 'Never' category, 17 per cent responded 'Occasionally' and around 3 per cent chose the 'Yes – a lot' category. Those respondents who reported bullying were also invited to include the names of any bullies – this produced some new information but no evidence to suggest that the pupil in question was upsetting any other of her peers.

Clearly, this last approach raises a variety of methodological issues, not least of which is the meaning which children attached to the word 'bullied', especially in those sub-cultures where solutions to interpersonal difficulties are more likely to be physical than verbal. In their investigation of this very point Arora and Thompson (1987) found that there was close agreement across pupils (aged 12 to 14 years) and teachers about the meaning of the word 'bullying' in the school which they studied.

A second issue relating to pupil-surveys concerns the extent to which children who are being bullied feel able to report this, even by anonymous questionnaire. Unfortunately, there is no conclusive way of comparing 'real' levels of bullying with levels reported in this survey although it is of interest that two of the youngsters who reported bullying wrote explicitly that they were unable to name the bully, presumably through fear of being found out and subjected to further harassment.

Whatever the quality and reliability of the specific and more general data yielded by this survey, there was a subsidiary hope on the part of the pastoral team that the pupils as a whole might feel an increased sense of security as a result of the interest shown by their teachers. It is, of course, quite possible that the very opposite may have resulted and that anxieties may have been increased by asking such questions. The parallels between bullying and child abuse are all too obvious, both of which phenomena rely for their potency to cause misery on secrecy and powerlessness. Wherever surveys are undertaken it is crucial to take account of those children not present at the time, especially in the light of suspicions that children who regularly miss school may be subjected to disproportionately high levels of bullying. It is a pity that the survey reported here was unable to throw any light on this contention.

Putting Together a Resource Pack

Having familiarised myself with what little literature was available in English I began to put together a draft Bullying Information Pack in 1987. I also set about consulting interested colleagues, teachers and other professionals working in the area of child-care. It was my intention to draw together theory and local experience to provide a starting point to be used by anyone working with children and that it would evolve in the light of 'consumer reaction'. The following material seeks to link a preventative, organisational approach with individual casework. The descriptive terms were selected cognisant of the dangers of 'labelling' and do not seek to marginalize children involved in bullying or present them as 'deviant'.

This is suggested as one route through what is potentially a complex piece of pastoral work. Self-evidently, it draws attention to the need for detail, clarity and the fullest possible sharing of information to provide a total picture of the problem. It is further emphasised that it is usually of

Figure 10.1 Bullying Action Plan

Identification

1. How did the problem come to light?
2. Who else might have relevant information and how might this be obtained?

Analysis

1. Who is directly involved in the bullying?

VICTIM

	sole individual	one of several	group
sole individual			
BULLY **one of several**			
group			

1. When, where and what form does it take?

Action

1. Have strategies been tried before – if so, what?

2. What appear to be the most important factors?
   (see checklists)

3. Details of new strategy (and review date)

great practical importance to clarify whether the youngster is involved on an individual basis or as one of a group: in this last case it is more likely that geographical, racial, religious or some other sub-cultural considerations are involved. It is also important to know whether a bully has one or more victims or, on the other hand, whether any particular individual is bullied by only one youngster or several others. Where this last situation is the case it is likely that any intervention should best be directed

...ds the victim as much as the bully. Incidentally, no apology is made / the use of the terms 'bully' and 'victim' although this is not to deny the highly interactional nature of human behaviour and the potential shown by many youngsters to act in both modes, the 'bully/victim' described by Stephenson and Smith (1988).

Figure 10.2

Factors Associated with Bullying: the Bully

Previous History

1	lack of success in school
2	above average physical size/strength
3	significant difficulties at home
4	parents encourage (perhaps covertly) this behaviour
5	parents unaware of the problem
6	encouraged by peers
7	history of bullying (perhaps often undetected)
8	admires older or 'higher status' people who bully
9	frequently sees bullying
10	history of being bullied
11	absence of negotiating skills
12	copes badly with anxiety
13	has difficulty expressing or controlling anger

Background (at the time)

14	absence/presence of adults
15	absence/presence of peers (who?)
16	not purposefully occupied/bored
17	feeling stressed/angry/anxious/frustrated/over-excited

Consequences – the 'pay off'

18	money, cigarettes, food, etc	Material
19	access to territory, games, seat, facilities, etc.	
20	peer approval/status	
21	feels accepted by social grouping, gang or cult – religious, racial, sporting, fashion, occupational	Social
22	maintains or improves self-image (e.g. 'tough' or 'powerful')	
23	heightened excitement or stimulation	Personal
24	reduction of stress/anger/anxiety/frustration	

other:

| | possibly | Name: .... |
| | very likely | d.o.b. .... |

This is a checklist comprising all the major factors hypothesised as being linked with children exhibiting bullying behaviour. It is emphasised that in any one instance only some of these will be present and the list is not intended as a definitive profile where all characteristics are anticipated. It is hoped that the act of filling out the checklist will be illuminating in itself but some suggestions and strategies are provided in the next section. For ease of exposition the factors are arranged in terms of history, background and consequences but the focus is much broader than the traditional, behaviourist one implied by this useful format.

The range of approaches set out in figure 10.3 is culled from a variety of sources which are feasible in school to a greater or lesser extent. Those which are too obviously impractical for teachers in terms of time or special expertise required have been omitted. When their views were canvassed, several professionals immediately suggested bringing bully and victim together almost as a matter of routine. It may well be though that this is posited on the fallacious assumption that the youngsters have a specific disagreement to resolve and the conciliation can be achieved via mediation. On the other hand, such a bringing together may serve to provide the bully with clear feedback about the distress which is being caused and might even act as a form of 'desensitization' to reduce the victim's upset or bring some reality to their fantasies.

Figure 10.3

Practical Strategies Focused on the Bully

Many children who bully will be experiencing significant emotional and personal difficulties at the time: on the other hand, many will not. It may be helpful to regard this behaviour as something which has been 'socially learned' and in the right circumstances may be 'unlearned'. Presumably chronic bullies went unchallenged for too long, were unable to learn from past interventions or still have too much to gain from their aggressive activities.

The traditional response of *punishment* may be counterproductive in that it relies heavily on a high level of detection and a threat of unpleasantness which outweighs the 'benefits' accrued from bullying. This limited approach may further reduce an already low self-esteem or increase feelings of powerlessness. Lastly, punishment may very well have the effect of increasing the bully's dislike of the victim(s), teacher(s) and school.

General Guidelines

1. Adults should react quickly, consistently and to every known instance.
2. Disapproval should be vigorous and unambiguous. Thought needs to be given to the timing and nature of the 'challenge' to maximise its impact. For example, the presence of parents at this time may lead to increased effectiveness or, on the other hand, they may instinctively defend the youngster or give 'mixed messages'.
3. Attention should be directed at the unwanted behaviour and not the person.
4. Alternative ways of behaving should be made available to the bully.
5. Parents should be involved in a constructive way.

Strategies

History

- Offer a wide range of leisure activities, where necessary involving excitement or a 'macho' element, leading to feelings of competence.
- Maximise feelings of success by a good curricular match.
- Explore family attitudes, enlisting expert help if appropriate in the form of family therapy.
- Teach relaxation skills.
- Facilitate expression of feelings via creative arts or drama.
- Set up a Social Skills group.
- Provide examples of admired people who do not bully (e.g. local celebrities).
- Set up a group/school project to promote awareness and change behaviour (e.g. via posters or video).
- Enable more constructive interactions between actual or potential bullies and victims via cooperative tasks. Older youngsters may 'befriend' newcomers to the school, help with leisure activities or in other curriculum areas ('peer tutoring').
- Provide specific educational input to counter cultural, religious or political prejudice.

Background

- Consider segregation at breaktimes or between lessons. Stagger the timing of the school day.
- Increase supervision - 'report' system or contract.

- Provide interesting breaktime activities.
- Look closely at the pattern of supervision, the layout of the school and rules relating to access.
- Consider possible environmental effects on aggressive behaviour (e.g. movement, noise, light, access to facilities, access to food and drink, design of furniture, etc.).

Consequences

- Encourage peer disapproval.
- Provide clear feedback on the extent of the distress caused.
- Insist on restitution in terms of repair or damage, finance or assistance.
- Set up an 'anti-bully squad' of older or more responsible youngsters. Conversely, give the task to youngsters who have themselves been involved in bullying (risky but potentially rewarding!).
- Provide specific counselling, especially 'verbally mediated control' (the youngster is helped to verbalize his/her actions, the outcomes and to identify alternative ways of behaving).
- Seek out and reward non-bullying behaviour:

  (a) informally
  (b) using targets, contracts, charts, token economy, etc.
  (c) provide positive feedback to parents via a letter or diary
  (d) set up a commendation book for children to praise peers who have become more sociable themselves or helped to prevent bullying
  (e) set up a competition between groups or individuals to reduce bullying – this might involve striking visual feedback in the form of large displays or charts.

Since drawing up this list of strategies I have become aware of some interesting work at a local Day Treatment Centre run by a Child and Family Therapy Team. Here children of up to 12 years of age come together from local schools in groups of four or five for one day per week to address a range of personal adjustment difficulties. In these intimate groups the staff undertake work on bullying from time to time in an attempt to better prepare the youngsters for life in their own particular school. One technique is to ask the children to nominate other members of the group whom they suspect may be bullies or victims in their school, rather like a simple sociogram, and then to use this information to prompt group discussion. In a safe environment children are helped to face up to their peer's suggestions about how or why they may be involved in bullying. There is also extensive use of video cameras involving role-reversals to help children appreciate other viewpoints or to practice what is in effect simple mediation, assertiveness or avoidance. It must be said that there are considerable reservations about the effectiveness of most conventional social skills training programmes. At the very least, though, these uses of video enable the children to begin to talk about their experiences. In a similar vein, the children are given oppor-

Figure 10.4

Factors Associated with Bullying: the Victim

Previous History

1	lacks close friends/unpopular with peers
2	physically less attractice/odd appearance
3	unusual social behaviour/mannerisms
4	over-passive/socially unassertive
5	family unpopular in the community
6	history of poor attendance
7	previously bullied
8	poor games skills/lacks co-ordination
9	provokes bullying (e.g. by name-calling)

Background (at the time)

| 10 | did not take reasonable steps to avoid location where bullying likely to occur |

Consequences

| 11 | unable to confide in trusted adult |
| 12 | suffered longer-term distress, e.g. anxiety, unhappiness, deterioration in school work, school refusal |

other:

| | possibly |
| | very likely |

Name: ....

d.o.b. ....

Figure 10.5 Practical Strategies Focused on the Victim

History

- Introduce new leisure activities in an attempt to boost confidence and popularity – you may need to consider alternatives in P.E. and Games.
- Provide assertiveness training, drama work or role play to improve confidence and practice specific social skills.
- Offer goal-directed counselling, especially with regard to personal appearance and 'avoidance of danger'. (e.g. 'Steps to Success' by John Thacker. N.F.E.R.-Nelson).
- Explore ways of improving popularity; younger children could bring a pet or possession into school or perhaps be given a 'high status' job in the classroom. The child could appear to win some privilege for the whole group as a result of his/her achievements or, on the other hand, suggest a popular activity or visit which is taken up by the teacher. (Clearly, these require a great deal of tact!).
- Actively involve the Education Welfare Officer.
- Explore what local agencies have to offer.

Background

- Positive segregation at breaktimes, allow to leave school early, change buses, change teaching group, etc.
- See strategies re bully.

Consequences

- Improve methods of detection (see 'Good Practice for Prevention' XII).
- Carefully monitor attendance and act quickly in the event of absence.
- Desensitization i.e. a meeting or joint activity with the bully in a carefully controlled situation.
- Set up a support group of victims to provide mutual, emotional comfort.
- Ensure easy access to pastoral staff – this may require regular contact to be initiated by a specific teacher. Practice 'active listening' techniques.
- Some children may require non-verbal ways of expressing their concerns (e.g. creative or practical activities).
- Maintain contact with parents – not just at times of crisis.

tunities to fantasise about the best and worst characteristics of school life and to act out these parodies in front of the camera.

An alternative to group work is individual counselling. A simple flow-chart which an adult might use as a basis for counselling a child who is being bullied or perhaps an older youngster may even use with a friend, has been found to be useful.

126

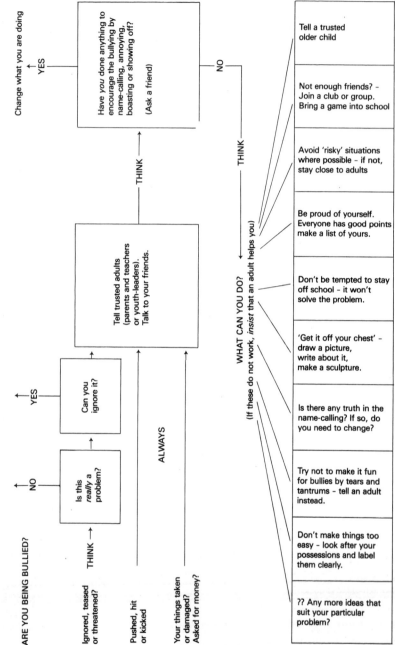

Figure 10.6

ARE YOU BEING BULLIED?

Ignored, teased
or threatened?

Pushed, hit
or kicked

Your things taken
or damaged?
Asked for money?

THINK →

Is this
really a
problem?

NO

Can you
ignore it?

YES

Change what you are doing

YES

Have *you* done anything to
encourage the bullying by
name-calling, annoying,
boasting or showing off?

(Ask a friend)

THINK

Tell trusted adults
(parents and teachers
or youth-leaders).
Talk to your friends.

ALWAYS

NO

THINK

WHAT CAN YOU DO?
(If these do not work, *insist* that an adult helps you)

Tell a trusted
older child

Not enough friends? –
Join a club or group.
Bring a game into school

Avoid 'risky' situations
where possible – if not,
stay close to adults

Be proud of yourself.
Everyone has good points
make a list of yours.

Don't be tempted to stay
off school – it won't
solve the problem.

'Get it off your chest' –
draw a picture,
write about it,
make a sculpture.

Is there any truth in the
name-calling? If so, do
you need to change?

Try not to make it fun
for bullies by tears and
tantrums – tell an adult
instead.

Don't make things too
easy – look after your
possessions and label
them clearly.

?? Any more ideas that
suit your particular
problem?

A HIGGINS and S PRIEST 1988

Running Workshops

From the outset my colleague, Andrea Higgins, and I were well aware that irrespective of the content of a Resources Pack or training initiative and the consideration of anticipated outcomes for the participants in terms of awareness, knowledge or new skills, at least equal attention must be given to the process of dissemination. We therefore regarded our early efforts as experimental and took careful note of the effectiveness or otherwise of the processes involved. We ran our first Workshop for 15 secondary school teachers from a variety of different schools in the area in 1988. Since then we divide up each session to reflect the dual approaches of a whole-school, *preventative* focus and, on the other hand, a *reactive* problem-solving response to specific incidents. For this second approach we have adapted a case-study from real life which highlights many of the most important issues and can be used to introduce participants to elements of the Bullying Information Pack.

Several Workshops on we are still using essentially the same format and case-study – this latter appears to have struck a note of familiarity for nearly all of the Workshop participants reminding us once more of the commonality of the issues involved. The point has been made many times that pastoral staff have the often difficult job of deciding which apparently trivial incidents may in fact be much more devastating in their consequences, judgements which may be made at speed, under duress or with little information to hand. In the sessions there is considerable interest in different styles of pastoral organisation, communication and record keeping to maximise support offered to children as well as the efficient collection of information. Inevitably discussion about the case-study leads away from 'crisis management' and on to a whole-school approach involving considerations of policy, ethos and organisation.

This paper has described a range of practical approaches to bullying in one part of the country. Although this initiative is still in its infancy, one way forward seems to be to arrange opportunities for teachers to reflect upon their work and share good practice. The most striking conclusion from this project so far is that whenever bullying occurs the adults involved in responding to the problem should begin by looking very closely indeed at their own attitudes to the incident and the children involved. From talking with a wide variety of professionals and parents there seems to be a marked ambiguity in our attitudes towards bullying which needs to be resolved if children are to be offered the guidance and protection to which they are entitled.

Figure 10.7

Bullying: Lisa and Julie

As the Head of 3rd Year I first met Lisa and Julie when they transferred to the Upper School last year. At first Lisa impressed as a well adjusted, if slightly shy youngster with a small but steady group of friends. However, during the Summer term her attendance deteriorated rapidly to the extent that the Education Welfare Officer made several visits. It was during one of these that Lisa's mother complained bitterly about longstanding bullying from Julie, something of which I had been quite unaware.

Towards the end of term I spent several sessions with Lisa who seemed genuinely frightened by Julie, appearing quite petrified when Julie looked at her in a certain way. At this stage Julie had never even touched Lisa to my knowledge but several other girls were passing messages to Lisa that Julie would 'do her' at the end of school – this she never did.

As school broke up in July, I heard from Matron that Lisa had spent many tearful sessions with her complaining about Julie throughout the year. When I searched through Lisa's school records I noted that her attendance had always been poor and, in fact, there had been quite a prolonged period of school-refusal at the end of her 1st Year, at which time she had also been complaining of bullying! I noted that Julie had only arrived at this school at the end of the 2nd Year.

When school re-started in September '88 Lisa adamantly refused to leave home in the morning despite two further visits from the EWO. It is now the fifth week of term and Lisa has not appeared.

Whereas Lisa comes from a conventional mining family of two parents and three elder siblings, Julie has had a troubled life and currently lives with her father since her mother died. She transferred to us two years ago following some sort of difficulty at her last school, the details of which were never passed on to me. Straight away Julie impressed as a tough character who soon became the leader of a mildly delinquent group of girls always ready to test the school rules to the limit. I am not sure whether she has close friends but she certainly has plenty of admirers. Material conditions at home are obviously poor and she fends for herself in most circumstances. Although I have not met her father, the EWO reports that he has a chronic health problem and finds it very hard to manage the household. He is believed to be a heavy drinker and there has been some concern expressed by the Social Services Department about Julie's welfare. She has five elder brothers who are known to the Police who visit the household from time to time.

I have spoken with Julie on many occasions over the last term and a half, during which time she has vehemently denied any antagonism towards Lisa. Until very recently staff have not reported to me any noteworthy incidents. For her part, Lisa continues to refuse to attend school until Julie leaves, repeatedly mentioning the 'looks' that Julie gives her.

There was just one incident in mid-July which was rather more tangible when Julie was seen to elbow Lisa in the corridor. In the light of Lisa's concerns, which extended even to threats of suicide, I had no option but to recommend that Julie be excluded for a few days and the Head agreed.

The current position is that Lisa is now refusing to attend school and only yesterday a friend of hers came to me complaining that Julie had now turned her attention away from Lisa and on to her.

Where do I go from here?

Figure 10.8

A Whole-School Approach to Bullying:
Good Practice for Prevention

I Bullying given a high priority (e.g. senior staff take an immediate personal interest).
II Any formal policy to be drawn up co-operatively by representatives of all interested parties to encourage feelings of 'ownership'. Such a policy to be fully and clearly communicated.
III Rapid and vigorous response to any incident.
IV Pastoral system well organised to facilitate effective communication and the sharing of information.
V Pupils feel able to approach staff to discuss problems and be heard sympathetically.
VI School ethos of tolerance and consideration for others.
VII Carefully considered pattern of supervision by staff with regard to the layout of the school. Unsupervised and isolated areas kept to a minimum.
VIII Curricular approaches to bullying (e.g. P.S.E., Humanities, expressive Arts, co-operative learning).
IX Close links with parents and Community.
X Pupils and parents explicitly reassured, especially at 'high anxiety' times (e.g. entrance, transfer to Upper School). Fears are usually excessive and unrealistic.
XI School takes responsibility for pupils 'in transit'.
XII Accurate assessment of the size and nature of the problem via systems for monitoring and consulting with pupils, parents and staff (e.g. informal conversations, tutor group discussions, meetings, questionnaires, attendance checks and indirectly e.g. via the creative arts curriculum).

References

Arora, C.M.J. and Thompson, D.A. (1987) 'Defining Bullying for a Secondary School' DECP. Educational and Child Psychology Vol. 4 Nos. 3 & 4, 1987.
Stephenson, P. and Smith, D. (1987) 'Anatomy of a Playground Bully' Education. Sept. 18. 1987.

CHAPTER 11

Resolving classroom conflicts non-violently

Jamie Walker

Conflict management is one of the major tasks of a teacher. Whether it is a relatively minor matter of children bickering with each other or disturbing a lesson, or a more serious case of bullying, teachers are constantly called upon to help children settle their differences. In this article I will discuss how the methods of non-violent conflict resolution can be used as a means to prevent children (and teachers) from solving their interpersonal problems in such a way that others are physically or emotionally harmed.

Bullying is only one example of unsuccessful or destructive conflict resolution. In a sense, the act of bullying itself serves as a substitute conflict. In most cases the real causes of the conflict lie within the bully her/himself, or – in the larger context – within the society which creates in some children the need to put others down. Let us take the case of a boy who lacks self-confidence (perhaps he has been beaten, ignored or in some other way mistreated at home) and resorts to bullying other children in order to assert his feeling of self-worth. This means that he creates problems for others in order to prove the fact of his own existence and power. But bullying other children will not, in the long run, help him to overcome his negative image of himself. Neither is it likely to contribute to any solution of the victim's real problems. On the surface it may appear that the bully is winning (at least until his destructive behaviour is interrupted) and the victim is losing, but I would assert that in reality both are losing and nothing is being done to get to the heart of the matter.

There are many other examples of violent and aggressive behaviour among children in the classroom and on the playground. Teachers, parents and school authorities are increasingly disturbed by the inability and/or unwillingness of children to solve their conflicts constructively. But what alternatives are children being offered? It is clear that moralising, i.e. telling them they shouldn't hit each other, will not bring long-term results. While it is undoubtedly necessary to set behavioural standards and enforce rules in a fair manner, it is just as essential to discuss the reasons for such standards and, as adults, to model positive behaviour. A teacher who appeals to her pupils to talk out their differences rationally will not gain much respect if she/he turns right around to shout at a child who has made a mistake rather than looking for the causes of the problem and attempting to find an appropriate solution. Children are more likely to take each other and authority figures seriously if they feel that they themselves are treated with respect. The question as to how one can solve conflicts constructively should be an issue which the entire class – and indeed the entire school – discusses regularly.

Aspects of non-violent conflict resolution

But what exactly is non-violent or constructive conflict resolution? Before I go into detail it is necessary to define the most important terms referred to in this article.

Non-violence is a principle by which the use of violence in any form – be it on the personal, social or political level – is condemned. Advocates of non-violence attempt to find alternative solutions to problems but also to change the structures which have led to violence.[1] The Norwegian peace researcher Johan Galtung defines violence as the 'cause for the difference between the potential and the actual, between that which could have been and that which is'. In other words, a relationship or situation can be regarded as violent if a person is prevented from achieving her or his objective possibilities. This could mean that she/he must starve while others live in luxury, that she/he must go without an education although it would be possible to give equal education opportunities to everyone in the society, or that health services are only made available to select groups. Galtung also differentiates between personal and structural violence: whereas with the former the subject-object relationship is clear (violence is carried out on an individual or a group), the latter is an indirect form. Structural violence, or 'social injustice', is built into the system and often accepted as natural. (Galtung: Strukturelle Gewalt 1977 – pp. 12–18).

A conflict is a clash between two or more individuals or groups and can be carried out with violent means but does not have to be. Non-violent antagonists in a conflict search for solutions which will enable both sides to at least partially meet their own needs. On an interpersonal level, non-violent conflict resolution does not attempt to avoid conflicts – non-violence cannot be equated with passivity – but rather to deal with them consciously, constructively and imaginatively. The prerequisites for this are:

- the creation of a trusting atmosphere in which the personal worth of every individual is respected, regardless of her/his social, cultural or family background;
- the desire and ability to communicate openly with each other;
- the desire and ability to think critically and work together towards finding a common solution to the problem.

The goal of non-violent conflict resolution is to find a 'win-win solution': instead of the two parties struggling against each other, they struggle together to reach an agreement which will make their relationship more meaningful as opposed to damaging it. Understood in this way, conflicts can be regarded as an opportunity rather than a threat. Of course, it is not always possible to arrive at mutually beneficial solutions, especially when the power in a relationship is unequally distributed or when one side refuses to even recognise the fact that a problem exists. However, all interpersonal conflicts grow out of the fact that individuals live, work or spend leisure time together and usually everyone involved has an interest in making the relationship 'work'.

Learning to deal with conflicts in this way is not an easy undertaking and, at least initially, can appear to 'cause' more trouble than it alleviates. I recently spoke with a secondary school teacher in Britain who had given a course in assertiveness training at her school. Assertiveness is the ability to communicate one's needs and desires in such a way that the rights of both parties are respected, i.e. neither aggressively nor submissively. One result of the course was that a group of pupils had gathered up their courage and resources to go and complain to another teacher. This teacher, of course, then became angry at the teacher who had taught the pupils to stand up for their rights in the first place, since it meant that she was forced to question her own actions!

It is clear, then, that teachers cannot be expected to 'teach' children the methods of non-violent conflict resolution if they themselves are not given the opportunity to be confronted with their own behaviour in relation to communication and problem solving in the classroom. It is also clear that this concept offers no instant or easy-to-follow recipes for solving conflicts the moment they arise. The idea that one should respect oneself and others is so simple and reasonable that no one could possibly disagree with it. But every teacher knows that the process of developing such respect in a classfull of lively children, each with their own individual backgrounds and problems, is long and hard. It is a process which involves affective as well as cognitive elements (especially with primary school children), and which demands that the teacher make an effort to deal fairly and equally with all pupils, regardless of her/his personal likes and dislikes.

One very common problem in schools is that of one-way communication. Both teachers and children frequently feel subjected to the institution which brings them together. Most decisions in schools are made in such a way that children are not asked what or how or when they would like to learn – and when they are asked they are usually unable to reply since they are used to being told what to do. Teachers experience pressure from above and below: they must adhere to the given structures (such as curriculum and note-giving) whether or not they are in agreement with them. In teaching the required material they often experience resistance on the part of their pupils. The pupils are dependent on the teacher to give structure and content to the school day, but the teacher is also dependent on the pupils to co-operate, at least to the extent that the lesson can be carried through. Many teachers spend as much or more time disciplining than actually 'teaching' – and often for the simple reason that the pupils are bored. Both sides feel that they are subjected to unfair treatment by the other and it is all too easy to let things run on as they are, hoping they will not get worse, rather than attempting to define, analyse and cope with the problems together.

One of the most important aspects of non-violent conflict resolution is open-mindedness or critical thinking. This involves not only the ability to approach a conflict with an open and critical mind, but also the willingness to change one's opinions in the face of new information or an increased understanding of a particular situation. Again, this is a very difficult task, as many people tend to enter a conflict situation with a particular standpoint or solution in mind which they are reluctant to question. While there is nothing wrong with having and expressing one's own position (indeed, it is difficult to carry out a conflict in which the positions are unclear), a lack of openness on one side or the other will more than likely prevent a truly common solution from being found. This, in turn, will negatively affect the implementation of the solution, since the one side did not really favour it in the first place.

The ability to question oneself and communicate with others effectively assumes the ability and willingness to express one's views and feelings openly and to listen attentively to those of others. 'Listening' is another one of those concepts which is, in my opinion, widely misunderstood. Most people interpret listening to mean the act of keeping one's mouth closed until the other person has finished what they are saying. (How often are children told: 'Be quiet and listen!') Instead of really trying to understand someone's problem and the feelings involved i.e. listening not only to the words but also to the meanings behind them, we often jump to our own conclusions about a particular situation and offer solutions few consider appropriate. Another misconception we have about listening – especially in conflict situations – is that listening to someone implies that you agree with them. If I am too busy gathering my own thoughts as 'ammunition' I will not be able to hear what the other person is saying. On the other hand, if I know that they will be willing to 'hear me out' when the time comes, I can afford to concentrate on what they are saying. Like any other aspect of conflict resolution, listening is an exercise in mutual understanding – and one which must be practised over and over again to be mastered.

Just as essential as listening in a conflict situation is the willingness to give and accept fair criticism and to admit doubts and failure. Many conflicts are based on a lack of communication and can be cleared up by simply discussing the matter in detail. Of course, even for this to happen a basic trust level must have been established, otherwise the participants will (rightly) refuse to expose themselves for fear of being unnecessarily hurt. This is especially true in the case of conflict partners who have avoided being open with each other up to that point. The longer a conflict is avoided, the more explosive it becomes and the more likely it will destroy or very nearly destroy the relationship. As the case with bullying, many people tend to engage in 'substitute conflicts': they avoid the real issues because they are too afraid of the consequences of confronting them head-on. The result is usually a gradual process of wearing down the relationship.

The last aspect of conflict resolution which I wish to mention before returning to the discussion of schools is that of imagination or creativity. One of the best ways to relieve tension during a conflict situation – once those involved have agreed on a common definition of the problem – is to brainstorm possible solutions. In this process it is essential to let one's imagination 'run wild', i.e. not to censor certain ideas from the start as being unreasonable or unacceptable (except for the possible ground rule that no solution may involve hurting any of the participants). This often results in laughter and the realisation that there is not necessarily one 'right' answer to the problem but many possibilities to chose from together. The better the individuals co-operate in finding a mutually satisfactory solution, the more likely the solution is to succeed. It is important to agree on trying out a particular solution for a set length of time, evaluate it and, if necessary, return to the idea list to find a new solution, etc. Of course, there are some situations in which it is virtually impossible to find a (positive) solution and one is forced to accept the facts as they are.

Teaching and learning conflict resolution skills: the co-operative classroom

Let us now turn to the question as to how the ideas presented above can be applied to the classroom situation. In this context I would like to introduce the concept of the 'co-operative classroom', one in which the groundwork for non-violent conflict resolution is being laid. The goal of creating a co-operative classroom can be approached in several different ways. The teacher can keep this goal in mind when planning lessons and other regular class activities, e.g. by having children sit in groups or a circle rather than in rows (if this is not already done), by having them work together in pairs or small groups during lessons, or by undertaking projects which involve independent group work. Care must be taken here to help children learn the true meaning of co-operation: just having them sit in close physical proximity to one another – even if it is a circle – does not necessarily mean that they are working together in the sense of creating something as a group which could not be created by the individuals involved.

Co-operation can best be understood by experiencing it on an affective level and then evaluating that experience on a cognitive level. The second approach, then, is to practise co-operative games and exercises in the classroom on a regular basis. Putting aside a special time each week to deal with these issues will provide a structure for co-operative learning which can later be extended to other classroom or school activities. It is intended that through such activities a situation will develop in which the teacher will not always be the centre of attention. Instead, the emphasis is put on the group, of which the teacher is a part (albeit a special one), as the pupils gradually learn to manage their own affairs. This does not mean that the teacher's authority should be undermined but rather that she/he becomes the pupils' partner in the process of learning, of learning to co-operate and solve conflicts non-violently. By being open to learning from the children, the teacher will model the same behaviour she/he is expecting of them. This will also avoid making the pupils dependent on the teacher's presence to put what they have learned in the classroom to use outside.

To summarise, the abilities and skills to be developed in the co-operative classroom are:

- self-respect and respect for others;
- communication;
- assertiveness;
- open-mindedness and critical thinking;
- empathy;
- co-operation;
- non-violent conflict resolution.

In order to illustrate how teachers can help children learn these skills I would like to describe some of the activities I use in my in-service teacher-training courses which the participants in turn employ in their class-rooms. Most of the exercises listed here have been developed by British and US American Quakers, who have been involved in the area of problem solving in schools since the early 1970s.[2]

Improving children's self-image

A child who's self-image is negative or who is not getting the positive attention it needs at home or in the school is more likely to disturb normal classroom activities. This will usually represent an attempt to call attention to itself, since negative attention is felt to be an improvement over none at all. On the other hand, a child who feels good about her- or himself can more easily concentrate on learning and will get more out of a lesson. Since children's levels of intelligence and talent vary, it is impor-tant to help each child find her/his strong points and to make sure that these strong points are recognised by all. Those children who are so enthusiastic that they tend to oppress others will need to learn to hold themselves back. One way of working on the problems of shyness, negative behaviour and over-enthusiasm is by playing games which affirm the inherent worth of every child. It is important that children are not forced to participate in activities if they feel too shy or embarrassed: usually they will want to participate after seeing that the games are not only non-threatening but also fun. The children will enjoy the games even more if the teacher participates.

Especially at the beginning of a school year it is important to spend time on activities which facilitate the process of getting to know each other and growing into a learning community. Teachers can lead name games, such as going around in a circle, saying one's name and adding an adjective which begins with the same letter or a movement which must be repeated by all, or throwing a ball of wool back and forth to form a net while repeating the names. Children can interview a partner (with or without set questions) and introduce her/him to the rest of the group. They can make name tags with a picture or a phrase describing something they like about themselves. They can design t-shirts and make notebooks or collages expressing positive aspects of themselves. One activity many teachers employ regularly is having pupils sit together in a circle in the mornings to relate 'news and goods' – exciting things which have happened since the class last met.

In evaluating such exercises children can be encouraged to talk about how it feels to say positive or derogatory things about themselves and others (i.e. which is easier? why?), what the difference is between bragging and being aware of one's good points, and why some people are particularly good at affirming others. As with all the other exercises and games described here, it is important to repeat the same type of activity on a regular basis.

Encouraging communication

Communication activities are those which aim to help children become aware of how effectively they normally communicate with each other and with adults and how they can improve these skills. The teacher can begin by having pupils listen to sounds inside and outside the classroom for one or two minutes and describe what they have heard. In a relaxation exercise children are asked to find a quiet place (real or imaginary) where they feel comfortable, alone and at peace with themselves; this can be a place they return to in their minds again and again, especially when they are feeling angry or upset. Other listening exercises include role play, brainstorming and discussion of good and bad listening responses and practising active listening in pairs by using pictures as a topic of discussion or talking about a recent experience. Older pupils can be given colourful cardboard shapes such as squares and triangles to be put together as designs and described to a partner who must make the same design without looking; this exercise will stimulate discussion on the fact that what seems perfectly clear to one person (e.g. directions) can mean something completely different to another. Further questions for the evaluation of communication exercises could include: How often do you really feel listened to? How does it feel? How often do you really listen to other people? Is this important? Why or why not? It should be made clear that communication is an essential element of co-operation and conflict resolution.

Developing assertiveness

The idea of assertiveness (i.e. getting one's needs met without hurting the other person) will be new to most children and some teachers. The class should discuss – perhaps on the basis of stories they have read together – what assertive behaviour involves and how it differs from aggressive or passive behaviour. How can one best stand up for one's rights? What is the effect of threatening someone (being aggressive) or failing to voice one's wishes effectively (being passive)? How can one identify one's own needs and desires and those of others? It is possible to satisfy both at the same time? What role does power play in relationships? Fear? Pupils should be asked about their own positive and negative experiences of standing up for their rights, e.g. with their parents, siblings, friends or at school. Have these strategies been successful? How could they be improved? In role plays they can practise being assertive (or 'diplomatic') and perhaps gain a better understanding of the advantages and disadvantages of this approach. Another topic for discussion in this context could be the question of how decisions are made in groups, including the class itself. What does the process of democratic decision making involve? How can a group weigh the ideas and desires of individuals against those of the group itself? Pupils (and the teacher!) will need to re-examine their everyday behaviour in light of what they have learned.

Learning open-mindedness and critical thinking

This goal will require the class to do a number of creativity exercises aimed at establishing the idea that there is not necessarily only one right or good solution to a problem but rather may be many possible solutions, depending on the imagination of the participants. The topic could be introduced by brainstorming a list of as many uses of an everyday object as possible, e.g. a paper clip or a belt. In most cases pupils will come up with a surprising number of ideas. Developing critical thinking also involves the ability to 'put yourself in the other person's shoes'. This can be illustrated by reading aloud a well-known fairy tale from the perspective of the underdog, as Little Red Riding Hood related by the wolf (whose house/forest was invaded by a little girl in suspicious-looking red clothes who even dared to insult his looks), and discussing the differences in the point of view from that of the better-known version. Children can then be asked to write their own fairy tales or stories.

A further point for discussion and role play will be the issue of criticism: How does it feel to give criticism? receive it? How can one criticise fairly and under which circumstances is it advisable to refrain from criticising? It should be made clear that learning to give and accept fair and relevant criticism is an essential component of constructive problem solving.

Developing empathy

Again, the discussion here centres around gaining a deeper understanding of individuals and the reasons for their particular attitudes and behaviour. The teacher could take the example of someone who is called upon to fulfill a number of different roles in her/his life (i.e. in the family, at work, with the neighbours) and describe how that person is viewed by those who know her/him. This can lead to consideration of what qualities one cherishes in others and what it means to be friends with someone. Children need to think about how they can learn to be considerate of people they do not like.

Practising Co-operation

As I mentioned earlier, the most important task here is to facilitate the experience of children working towards a common goal, if possible one that has been set by themselves. The teacher can begin by playing simple but games such as 'knots': participants stand in a circle with their eyes closed, grab two other hands from the middle, open their eyes and attempt to get back into the circle without letting go of each other. In 'human machines' small groups pantomime a machine of their choice for the rest of the class to guess; a variation of this is for everyone to form one giant imaginary machine together. 'Co-operative laps' is an alternative version of the traditional game musical chairs: instead of sitting on chairs when the music stops (and someone losing out every round), participants walk around in a tight circle and attempt to sit on the person's lap behind them as soon as the music is over. With 'touch blue' objects or colours such as 'jeans', 'watch' or 'red' are called out and everyone must touch that on someone else. The purpose of all these activities is that everyone has an equal chance of ending up the centre of attention and that when no one loses everyone wins.

Taking a blindfolded partner on a 'trust walk' (and changing roles afterwards) is another way of approaching the issue of co-operation. There are also a number of co-operative exercises involving non-verbal communication. The literature concerned with non-competitive and co-operative games and exercises for children is extensive. In the school situation, however, discussion should also centre around the question of when it is not a good idea to co-operate, i.e. you do not trust the motives of the person asking you to help them. This consideration, along with the discussion on standing up for one's rights, may help children avoid situations in which they could be mistreated.

Conflict resolution

By now it should be clear that through discussion and activity on the previous topics a solid basis has been established for approaching the issue of conflict resolution. Perhaps it is best to begin by asking children what kinds of conflict they are familiar with and where they have experienced positive and negative conflict resolution or problem solving. The teacher can bring stories or comics (the dialogues to be filled in by the children) into the class to stimulate further discussion and the pupils can brainstorm "prerequisites for successful conflict resolution". They can also make a list of common classroom conflicts, analyse their causes and implications and roleplay alternative solutions. It will probably be necessary to repeat the same role plays several times so that children receive the opportunity to experience the conflict from different perspectives and to develop realistic ideas as to how it can be resolved.

In a real conflict situation the participants should first try to agree on a definition of the problem, then talk about what it means to them personally, brainstorm possible solutions, agree on one and evaluate it after a set period of time. If necessary, they should later go back to the list of solutions and begin anew. Even with such practise in the classroom, the step towards applying what they have learned to outside situations will be a difficult one for most pupils, especially those who are receiving conflicting messages from their parents (i.e. 'If someone hits you, hit them back!'). This is all the more reason to make the issue a general topic of discussion in the school and with parents. The more support children get along these lines the better they will be able to break destructive behavioural patterns and develop constructive ones.

Conclusion

Social or political violence always involves an individual dimension. This dimension effects personal relationships by hindering communication or making it one-sided. In this case, one usually reacts to the violence and not to its causes. At school this means that disruptive behaviour is interpreted as being destructive and calls forth negative or frustrated reactions. But when violent or aggressive behaviour (such as bullying) on the part of children and young people is understood as a message, it would be important to find out exactly what that message is trying to convey.

Ignoring children's emotional needs serves to increase the potential for violence in the school. Many children suffer themselves from the aggressive atmosphere at school, although they contribute to it through their own behaviour. Schools are entrusted with the task of bringing up children in a moral sense as well as educating them in an intellectual sense – and they should be constantly reminded of this fact. Giving children the social skills they need to achieve their own potential is no less important than teaching them mathematics or history. Many teachers resign themselves to accepting aggressive behaviour on the part of certain pupils and are unable to break the cycle of violence, although it is up to them (and not the children) to do this. The goal of class and school activities along these lines is to transform the aggression, utilising the aggressive energy in a positive manner.

The school should attempt as far as possible to create an environment free of violent structures. Of course, it will be impossible to cut the school off from the outside world. But teachers and school authorities can be conscious of which structures are conducive to or defuse violent and aggressive situations and decide on possible changes in school policy. One example of this would be to institute a rule that hitting is not allowed in the school. Even if children hit each other on the way to or from school or at home, at least there is one place in their lives where they experience that this behaviour is unacceptable and they are forced to look for alternative solutions to their problems. Schools experimenting with such rules have discovered that a concerted effort of the whole staff is necessary to ensure success.

Bullying and related destructive behaviour indicates a need for increased attention to the affective aspects of education. I hope to have shown in this article that this cannot be only a matter of dealing with conflicts the moment they actually arise (and thus fulfilling the function of a fire brigade) but must be seen as an important preventative measure. By establishing a co-operative classroom atmosphere both children and teachers will be better able to cope with conflicts constructively and non-violently when they do arise.

142

References

1 Although in this article I confine myself for the most part to discussing the level of interpersonal conflicts, I do feel it is important to be aware of the fact that even personal conflicts have a social or political dimension. Changing children's behaviour will only be effective in a limited manner if the socio-political causes (such as limited or virtually non-existent education and job opportunities, or discrimination on the basis of race, sex, religion or nationality) of anti-social behaviour are not simultaneously dealt with.

2 For further information see: Kingston Friends Workshop Group: *Ways and Means – An approach to problem solving*, Kingston upon Thames 1985. Available from: Friends Book Centre, Euston Road, London NW1 2BJ. Also: Priscilla Prutzman, *et al.*: *The Friendly Classroom for a Small Planet – A Handbook on Creative Approaches to Living and Problem Solving for Children*, Wayne, New Jersey 1978 and Stephanie Judson (ed.): *A Manual on Nonviolence and Children*, Philadelphia 1977. Both available from: New Society Publishers, 4722 Baltimore Ave., Philadelphia, Pa. 19143.

CHAPTER 12

A System Oriented Strategy Against Bullying

Erling Roland

One can with great certainty maintain that at least 5% of the pupils in Scandinavian schools (grades 1–9) are systematically bullied and that at least the same amount of pupils are responsible for this.

The definition we use in our work is:

Bullying is longstanding violence, physical or mental, conducted by an individual or a group and directed against an individual who is not able to defend himself in the actual situation.

Bullying does not only concern the victims and the bullies, it also affects parents, teachers and peers who are all a part of the social system in which bullying occurs. In this chapter I will take a look at steps which can be taken to deal with bullying in this kind of a system perspective.

The model below illustrates the social system which will be discussed:

Figure 12.1 Model for system strategies to deal with bullying.

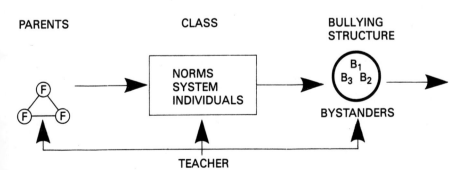

The strategies or steps which can be taken are presented as advice to the teacher in the above model.

The left-hand side of the model represents the parents/families (F) of the pupils in each class. Lines have been drawn to indicate the interaction which can take place between them. The middle part shows the class with its individual pupils (p), a social system and norms. On the right-hand side we find the group of bullies (B1-B4), the victim (V) and in addition the bystanders who observe what is going on. This social system including bullies, victim and bystanders is called the bullying structure.

As can be seen, lines have also been drawn from the parents to the class and from the class to the bullying structure to suggest links between these units.

Lines have also been drawn from the teacher to these units which are meant to illustrate that the teacher must see to these relations.

In my opinion, teachers must work in two ways when combatting bullying;

1.   Take general measures.
2.   Intervene when bullying is taking place.

I. General measures

In the following, I will present general measures which can be used when dealing with parents and with the class.

Parents:

On the left-hand side of the model, we find the pupils' parents. Lines have also been drawn between the families to illustrate how meaningful the relationship between them is. As a general strategy against bullying, I feel it is very important for the teacher to develop a close network between the families of the pupils in the class.

One knows that information flows more easily in close networks (Roland 1983). One must also assume that the pupils in the class are aware that this information exchange between the parents is going on and that the parents will thus have the opportunity to know what their children are up to. If the children know this, they will probably be more careful about their behaviour and not bully as much.

It is also known that closer networks between families tend to create common norms for child rearing (Abernethy 1973). If the children are aware of these common norms, this will also help to inhibit bullying behaviour.

During my many years of practical work with pupils, parents and teachers, I have also experienced that such a network is a great asset when bullying is actually taking place. Such a network makes it so much easier for the parents to get in touch with each other and thus be able to sort out problems on their own. It is also so much easier for the teacher to stimulate such cooperation if there already are good relations between the parents.

A major task for the teacher is then to create situations in which such a network can be developed. This work should start as early as possible, before any problems among the pupils appear. The first meetings the teacher has with the parents are opportunities to promote various ways to enable the parents to become acquainted. This can be done for instance by arranging informal meetings or outings for the parents so that they are given the opportunity to talk with each other.

I have also found it effective to use these meetings to discuss common norms which should govern the conduct of the pupils and the importance of exchanging information between the parents if and when any problems should arise, (for example, bullying among the children).

Finally, it is also of great importance for the teacher to emphasize good relations with all the parents so that information can flow between parents and teacher. This may lead to a positive relationship towards the school and may improve cooperation with the teacher. This can prevent bullying from occurring because the pupils notice that the parents and teacher inform each other and cooperate well.

The class:

In the model, the relations between the teacher and each pupil have been emphasized. If the teacher can develop relationships which are positive and many-sided with each pupil, this can be influential in many ways (Auestad et al. 1986). The teacher will achieve greater influence on each pupil. Also, this can improve the relationship between the pupils if they have a common figure of identification (Heider 1944; Simmel 1964). One must assume that both increased influence on the teacher's part and increased friendship among the pupils will contribute to preventing bullying from occurring.

In addition to paying attention to each pupil, the teacher should also work specifically on the social system of the class. In my opinion, a major goal for the teacher should be to develop an organisation where responsibility has been divided among the pupils. This can be achieved through establishing permanent groups in the class which are responsible for various tasks and for carrying out projects within the instruction given. The teacher should then aim at creating what can be called complementary groups which means that the pupils must depend on each other to carry out their task. Here it is essential that each pupil is given tasks which he or she really is capable of fulfilling. This will probably contribute to social integration in the group and also to increasing the respect for each pupil.

How responsibility is measured out within a group could include having one person as the leader of the group. This leadership function is one that can alternate among the group members. The organisation can be further developed to include regular meetings between the teacher and the leaders of each group with an object to coordinate the activities in each group. Thus, also the groups become dependent on each other. Such mutual dependency at various levels in the class will probably stimulate the growth of friendship between the classmates and friendship can be difficult to combine with bullying.

At this point it must also be stressed that norms will always be developed in a class. This is also one area in which the teacher can have his/her say.

If the teacher is able to create positive relations with each pupil, then it will be possible for the teacher's own behaviour and attitude to have an effect on the pupils (Bandura 1977). In addition, the organisational model described above will encourage the growth of common norms of social behaviour (Heider 1944, 1946, 1958; Simmel 1964).

It is of course also possible for the teacher to focus on actual norms which can be discussed in class. As I see it, it would then be wise for the teacher to first consider which norms are desirable and then discuss these with the pupils according to a thorough plan (Roland 1983).

It can be difficult to discuss something openly if the pupils are not well prepared. As a guideline, I would therefore suggest that the teacher first 'warms the pupils up' by introducing this theme in some way, for instance by showing a movie/filmstrip/slides series or by reading from a book on the topic. The pupils can also be asked to write something about this topic.

After this preparation it is usually easier to have a fruitful conversation with the pupils. One need not be afraid of discussing bullying and the agreed expectations which should be effective in dealing with this type of behaviour. Many teachers find it useful to have these agreed upon norms in a written form so that they can be visible for the whole class.

Conclusion:

As the reader has probably noticed, the main intention of the teacher's work sketched above has been to create a system of social integration between parents, pupils and the teacher. By social integration, I mean social systems where members act in mutual dependency according to agreed norms. When these norms are governed by the demand for prosocial behaviour, one would expect this to inhibit and limit bullying and that any bullying episodes would be easier to detect and handle.

II. Intervention

On the right-hand side of the model I have used the term 'the bullying structure'. By this I understand those pupils who are involved in bullying as bystanders, bullies and victims.

Teachers must know and understand the principles and methods for working with such a system.

The victim

When it is clear that bullying is taking place the teacher should first have a conversation with the victim. In my opinion, this would be the correct procedure because the vicim can otherwise feel overlooked or denied of his/her say in solving a matter that ultimately concerns and has an impact on the victim. One must remember that this child may have been in a situation where others have been in control of the child's life which may have been a harrowing experience. When the teacher starts this work to stop bullying by talking to the victim first, this is a way to signal that the child is part of solving the problem. The feeling of helplessness can then be broken. It is important to be aware that most victims are both afraid and reserved. Often they find it embarrassing to admit that they are being bullied by peers and they can also fear the consequences of doing something about it. At the same time, these children feel a strong need for help and compassion from the teacher.

It is not wise to beat about the bush in such conversations. This can make the pupil feel even more insecure. Instead, the teacher should say in a friendly but unwavering way, that he/she knows about the bullying and that he/she wants to cooperate with the victim to put an end to this. On the basis of considerable experience, I am sure that this is the way to win the pupil's confidence, and confidence in the teacher is vital for the progress one hopes to make. The teacher should also say that the pupil will be consulted with on all further steps. This will help reduce and eliminate uncertainty.

The victim must understand that this matter will be dealt with seriously and that the two of them will be meeting regularly for conversations about what to do.

Two principles for further work with the victim are briefly outlined below:

1. The teacher can try to help the victim cope with bullying situations in a better way. It is wise to start carefully. The teacher can for example advise the pupil to make contact with other 'less dangerous' pupils and discuss how this can be achieved. The pupil can attempt this contact and report on it during the next conversation. At this time, the two of them can agree on further steps. Eventually, one can approach the bullying situation itself and try to teach the pupil adequate ways of reacting. This can be important because many victims of bullying show exaggerated fear when provoked or other kinds of behaviour that can encourage the bullies. In addition to discussing these reactions, the pupil can practice them through role play with the teacher.

2. Another useful procedure is to encourage peers to be with the victim. One must then choose pupils who can be trusted and who have a certain influence on other pupils. The teacher may consider whether this should be arranged only for school hours or if this arrangement should be carried further. In the latter situation, this could be arranged to include time spent at youth clubs, sports clubs etc. where the teacher can cooperate with other adult leaders. One reason for establishing such ties is that through this, the victim achieves both social contact and protection.

The bullies

Before one gets in touch with the bullies, this should be aired with the victim. This is important so that the victim feels he knows what is going on.

Usually there are more children who get together to bully a school-mate. A golden rule is not to contact the whole group at once. In such a situation, the bonds between the members would be so strong that the teacher would get nowhere and accomplish nothing. (See also Pikas, in this volume).

Instead, the teacher should arrange for separate conversations with the bullies. He/she should make it clear that one knows about the bullying. The bully will feel some pressure at this time, and the time is ripe to invite him/her to cooperate in helping the victim. This can well be explained in a slightly flattering way, for example by complimenting the bully on good cooperation at an earlier time. In my view, this combination of determination and invitation is the best. Through this, one can both achieve getting the bully to stop victimizing others and to prevent further bullying.

This further work should be discussed briefly with the bully and can for instance include helping the victim if necessary.

Afterwards, similar conversations should take place with the other bullies. This can be done within one school period, one child after the other. A substitute must be arranged so that the bullies are not able to communicate with each other while these conversations are going on.

It is crucial that the teacher meets with the whole group of bullies after this sequence of conversations (Pikas 1976). One must then be aware that none of these pupils knows what the other has said and will therefore be a bit uneasy with each other. Therefore, the teacher must say what each has stated. Relief is obtained as they become familar with the fact that the others have agreed to cooperate with the teacher.

Future plans must become concrete and the teacher must not forget to set a new date for a new meeting. My experience shows that it is relatively easy to encourage cooperation from the bullies if one follows the steps mentioned above.

Still, as the pupils leave the teacher, one must assume that the event will be commented on amongst them, and this conversation need not be constructive! Often, pupils will now withdraw and perhaps try to ridicule the teacher and his/her proposition.

I have experienced that the following procedure can be fruitful (Roland 1983). The teacher can briefly say something about that he/she knows that they will talk about what has happened and continue: 'It might be tempting to walk out on the whole affair then. Will you do that? What about you, Paul, will you sabotage what we have agreed on? What about you, Chris?'

The teacher should also prepare the pupils for what will face them when they return to the class. 'When you meet the others in the class they will probably ask you what you have talked to me about. It might be tempting to sabotage our agreement then. What will you answer them, Eric?' The teacher may also give suggestions to what they can answer, for example that it is no one else's business.

Such a method has proven to be quite effective because it makes the pupils more prepared for the situation they will face when they leave the teacher, and it also gives the pupils a chance to agree on an answer.

The bystanders

As far as I know, no studies have been made on the interaction between the bullies, the victim and the bystanders when bullying is taking place. I will not speculate on the contents of this interaction, just point out that it is possible for the teacher to reach an agreement with pupils in the class not to stimulate the bullies but to rather defend the victim in such cases. In most of the cases where I used this strategy, the bullies then lost interest when they only attracted negative reactions from their peers. This is especially the case if the pupils who react negatively are the pupils who have the highest status in the class.

The parents

This brings us back to where I started; the parents. It is possible for the teacher to get in touch with both the parents of the the victim and of the bullies in order to discuss with each of them what can be done. This should happen after the teacher has talked with the children.

It can be especially effective if the respective parents can meet each other together with their children. Before such a meeting can take place, the teacher must have prepared the parents and the children in a very thorough way. It is vital that everyone understands that this meeting is not the time nor the place to accuse or attack each other about incidents that have occurred, but that they should rather use this meeting to discuss future solutions. Should the teacher be uncertain about whether or not such a meeting will be a success, the meeting should not take place. But if the teacher feels the parents and children are ready for this, and if the parents show that they are willing to cooperate and make demands on their children, it is quite unlikely that the bullying will continue.

Conclusion

Such a system-perspective on strategies against bullying is, according to my view the most functional in the long run, both to prevent and to intervene. Here we must, however, always keep in mind that the victim does not only have the right to be left in peace, but also has the right to be a part of the social system. This will demand consideration in addition to the work on preventing and stopping bullying.

References

Abernethy, V. (1973) Social Network and the Response to the Maternal *Role*. International Journal of Soc. of the Family, No. 3.

Auestad, T. (1986) *Jo mere vi har sammen*. Stavanger: Stavanger College of Education.

Heider, F. (1944) *Social perception and phenomenal causality*. Psychological Review 51, p. 358–374.

Heider, F. (1946) *Attitudes and cognitive organization*. Journal of Psychology 21, p. 107–112.

Heider, F. (1958) *The psychology of interpersonal relations*. New York: Wiley.

Pikas, A. (1976) *Slik stopper vi mobbing*. Oslo: Gyldendal.

Roland, E. (1983) *Strategi mot mobbing*. Oslo: Universitetsforlaget.

Roland, E. (1983) *Sosialt nettverk som pedagogisk begrep*. Stavanger: The Stavanger College of Education.

Simmel, G. (1964) *Conflict and the Web of Group-affiliation*. London: Collier-MacMillan.